21st Century's
New Chakra
Healing

21st Century's
New Chakra
Healing

Michael Nudel & Eva Nudel, Ph.D.

Bio-Energy System Services
Los Angeles, CA

21st CENTURY'S NEW CHAKRA HEALING

Disclaimer: This book is the result of research and experience of the authors, however it is not intended as a medical guide, nor is it to be interpreted or used as a substutute for a professional medical care. Consult your doctor for any serious health problems.

You are responsible for your own health and the health of your relatives. The publisher assumes no responsibility for the efficacy of these techniques, nor do the authors promise any cures. Use caution and common sense, and perform the exercises and techniques gradually.

Published by
Bio-Energy System Services
P.O. Box 461685, Los Angeles, CA 90046, U.S.A.
ISBN 0-9677514-1-1

Printed and bound in U.S.A.

To our children,
Julia, Meryl and Kevin

CONTENTS

IIIUSTRATIONS

Books by Michael and Eva Nudel
Health by Bio-Energy and Mind

HOW TO CONTACT THE AUTHORS

Michael Nudel and Eva Nudel, Ph.D., provide distant energy healing and bio-energy system assessment and services for individuals, organizations, and businesses. Requests for information and services should be directed to them at the address below. Readers of this book are also invited to contact the authors with comments and ideas for future editions.

Michael Nudel and Eva Nudel, Ph.D.
Bio-Energy System Services
P.O. Box 461685
Los Angeles, CA 90046

Web site: http://www.bioenergy-services.com
E-mail: healers@bioenergy-services.com
Books by the authors are available at Amazon.com.

Introduction

As small parts of the Universe, we must submit to the Laws of the Universe. People use five senses to perceive the material world around them. However, our material world consists of more subtle occurrences than can be perceived by the five senses, and if we become attuned to the higher dimensional worlds, we can more easily comply with the Laws of the Universe. In other words, by developing your ability to sense energetic fields, you will perceive the world around you with a more complete perspective that includes a newly developed bio-energetic ability.

This book presents a revolutionary method of chakra and bio-energy healing. This never-before published method of energetic cleansing, balancing, normalizing, and healing can be utilized by anyone to heal the self and others. While chakra healing has been used for thousands of years, I have synthesized these ancient teachings with my own techniques to form a unique and innovative method named *Ether "Double" Image Healing*. My book reveals this method of chakra energy healing, which may be performed by anyone, on anyone, and at any distance.

At birth, we are all given the unique ability to feel our own bio-energetic field and that of others, as well as the energy field of any live matter. People hold powerful energetic strength and potential, inside and out. This book will give you special techniques to open and develop bio-energetic ability and use it for your own health and balance. You will not only be able to help yourself be healthy, you can help family, loved ones, and pets as well. By learning to control and direct your own energy, or even the energy of anyone else, you will learn how to achieve optimum health for yourself and others.

I have been developing methods for bio-energetic and chakra healing for over twenty-five years. I have helped many people, and I continue my healing practice helping people in their healing process with my naturally strong bio-energetic field. In this practical handbook, I am passing on valuable discoveries made during my healer's experience.

Developing bio-energetic abilities is a fascinating and evolving process. Once you begin developing your energy and healing abilities, it is not possible to stop, turn away, or forget the experience. Once I started, I could never stop learning. I experimented with bio-energy and chakra healing, developing new methods and possibilities to heal and assess bio-energy. Thereafter, my deep understanding of human energy fields and energetic information, through intensive research and step-by-step experimenting in energy healing at close and long distance, have determined my new vision of employing bio-energy in the healing and balancing process.

Six years ago, I started performing an energy assessment and healing of bio-energetic systems in an absolutely new way. It all began when a man asked me to assess the energy state of another person who was far away. His photo was not available, and the man had never seen the person he was asking about, but he wanted to help his friend's loved one.

At that time, my healer's tools were my comprehensive methods of energy assessment and healing described in the book *Health by Bio-Energy and Mind*. I could assess the energy state of any person through a photo, or I could assess the energy through a mental image of the healee visualized by another person who knows the healee. But how could I assess the bio-energy of his friend's relative without a photo or energetic image, which had be constructed by me with the man's mental help?

As it turned out, that man (he was an artist) offered to draw the person. Whether it was the power of an artist's wish or his personal energy, I now had the confidence I needed to assess that unknown person. Though I could not draw a professional image, by using my imagery and letting my intuition flow, I drew a funny figure. When I passed my "activated" energetic hand over the image, I discovered energy in it. Intuitively, I realized the necessity to write the name and birthdate over the drawing to determine the person's energy. I imagined the person, acquiring his energetic image from the drawing, and put it before my eyes. Keeping the energetic "double" before my eyes, I assessed the unknown person's energetic state.

I was amazingly surprised with this event and new energetic work, and I began to frequently draw energetic images of my friends and relatives, always perceiving some energetic information from those drawings. Thereafter, my destiny brought me to a master of extrasensory perception, clairvoyance and numerology, a woman named Irina. She is a famous clairvoyant in Uzbekistan, our country of origin, and a wonderful person as well. When I told her my story, she took an extrasensory look at my drawings and offered to place chakras on them to perceive detailed energetic information from the energetic images. Irina helped me to complete my drawing up to its energetic perfection.

It was the beginning of a new way in chakra healing on the *ether "double" image*, which I have greatly developed and practiced over the years. Since then, I have drawn tens of thousands of energetic images, assessing people's energetic states and performing chakra healings. After years of persistent practice, I and my wife, Eva, have developed a synthesis of ancient knowledge about chakras and human energy with our own practice and bio-energetic methods. We have created a harmonious system of assessment and healing that is precise and easily performed.

We started writing our books to share with our readers unique and useful information about bio-energy healing and assessment of the energy systems. We are positive that more people will comprehend and start to be involved in bio-energy healing and balancing on an everyday basis. In our first book, ***Health by Bio-Energy and Mind***, we introduced our step-by-step program on how to start feeling bio-energy and to open and develop a bio-energetic ability to assess and heal our energy systems. This first book was the forerunner for this one. It was the first step to prepare the reader's consciousness for bio-energy and chakra healing and its techniques.

Only through reading the first book will a reader completely comprehend the methods and techniques of the present book.

People are energy beings. The roots of human problems are energy problems. Thoughts, emotions, feelings, and actions are energy actions. You influence other people with your bio-energy, and other people in turn influence you. Energy fields interact when people stay close to each other. When an influence is positive and peaceful, you gain positive energy and balance. On the other hand, when people are faced with an angry communicator or prolonged stressful event, they are involved in a negative energetic influence. In many cases, people's energy may be blocked, become unbalanced, stagnant or stale.

This book will teach you how to release energy blocks, whether they be emotional, mental, or even spiritual blocks, and to release bio-negativity in a new way never published before in bio-energetic and chakra therapy. You will be able to open your chakras and make them working and functional. Functional chakras bring vital energy to the chakra and energy system.

In addition, you will learn how to prepare your mind and your bio-energy to perform the bio-energetic healing work and maintenance of physical, mental, emotional, and energetic health on an everyday basis. You will learn how to achieve a meditative state of mind - an important healer's tool in energy and chakra healing. You will learn how to develop visual memory and the ability to visualize. A vast amount of healing work is performed with the help of visualization. Visualization may be healing in its nature, just as positive thought may be healing. Nevertheless, you will learn to use your newly developed ability to visualize in an absolutely new and unique way.

Finally, you will learn how to achieve an energetic balance in order to prevent physical illnesses, and to perceive positive healing information and discharge unwanted energetic information or harmful bio-negative energy from human energetic systems. You will be able to relieve imbalances and discomforts on the energetic and physical level. You will be able to use color and crystal chakra therapy on the ether "double" image in a new and innovative way that works to influence the physical state. And moreover, you will be able to maintain your healthy energy state and heal illnesses.

You do not need to be a specialist, psychic or healer to gain awareness from this book. Nevertheless, you may grow spiritually and energetically. Our teaching will give you the possibility of self-awareness, personal growth, wisdom, new understanding and maturity.

21st Century's New Chakra Healing will help you to be healthy and to live a highly energetic, distress-free, balanced life. You will improve your relationships and communication, learn to be more successful with high self-esteem and inner-self knowledge, and be happy and positive-minded. The unique method of ***Ether "Double" Image Chakra Healing*** can be your effective healer's tool forever. You need not believe my words, you will be able to know, practice and observe miracles of healing and energetic influence on your own. I believe my method of *Ether "Double" Image Chakra Healing* opens the door to the Future of Medicine: self-healing, health and energetic balance, and intuitive control over energetic or any kind of information and influence. Using the *ether "double" image method of chakra healing*, you will be able to find any imbalances and problems in your chakras and chakra system, your organs, body parts, and body systems. You will fix them all with ***21st Century's New Chakra Healing***.

–Michael Nudel

Chapter One

Subtle Bodies of a Cosmic Organism

Humans are complex energetic systems. People receive energy from the air and give it out in the form of thoughts, emotions, and actions. People have electromagnetic fields surrounding them a network of high and low bio-energy fields. These energy fields are both material and nonmaterial (as particles and waves or quanta). These fields consist of different energies, from dense physical energy to subtle energies which control many of the physical body's activities, characteristics, actions, feelings, or emotions. Slow-vibrating matter is considered to be physical matter, whereas the subatomic vibrating at the speed of light is a subtle matter, or energy. The physical body is penetrated by subtle vital energies as well as slow-vibrating matter.

All living things are surrounded with their own "atmosphere," which we refer to as the bio-energy field or aura. The **bio-energy field**, or **aura**, is different from any other known fields in physics. The aura is the summary of energy fields around the human body or any live object, and manifests as any radiation or radiance around material objects. (However, the aura cannot be seen by usual sight at usual terms.) Minerals, plants, animals, and humans all possess their own special aura. There is no dead material; all objects live, breathe, move, "laugh," and suffer.

Humans possess especially powerful bio-energy fields. From birth, people's bodies are wrapped by this "invisible" covering, which can be seen by clairvoyant people as a radiant, immensely colored or whitish haze. The bio-energy field cannot be seen around a dead body, because all subtle bodies, from which the bio-energy field consists, leave a dead body.

Aura means "breeze," "halo," and "light" in esoteric terms. Usually, the aura cannot be seen by ordinary people, only by spiritually sensitive people with the ability to perceive "invisible" energies. Nevertheless, sometimes this radiance becomes so bright that many people can see it. Psychics, sensitive people or clairvoyants, and hypnosis specialists are able to perceive aura in a trance state, but a trance state is not necessary for such perception. Many people can observe auras after being in a totally dark room for a few hours.

Humans radiate energy waves. When the mental activity of someone changes, these waves change also. Such modifications can occur with a speed of thought sent by a human. The aura or bio-energy field is a summary of human electromagnetic fields, all subtle bodies with their energetic potentials that give strength and power to the biological field. The aura plays the role of an energetic reservoir. Our energetic potential depends on conditions of physical, emotional and psychic health, generic baggage, and perhaps astrological factors as well. The bio-energy field consists of a few subtle energetic bodies, all different in structure, forms of energy, and distances of their extending from the physical body. These layers protect us as atmosphere protects the earth.

The subtle bodies that make up the bio-energetic field are complex structures as compared to the physical body. They associate with human emotions and thoughts as forms of human energy. Besides our physical bodies, we possess seven more "invisible" (at usual glance) subtle energetic bodies, all with their own individual "color" of energy that gives a personal tone of the aura to everyone. All subtle bodies are differentiated by density of their material and energy. These subtle bodies, or "seven human beginnings," range from the most dense - the physical body - to the most subtle in the following order: **Ether**, **Astral**, **Mental**, **Karmic**, **Intuitive**, **Nirvana**, and **Absolute**.

The material and energy of each of these subtle bodies differ from another just as gas differs from a solid matter. Such conditions as gas, fluid, and solid matter represent dense physical matter, whereas material and energy of all other subtle bodies belong to higher substances and energetic forms.

Before learning about bio-energy healing and methods, you will need to understand the seven subtle human bodies that make up the bio-energy field.

Ether Body

The **ether body** is an **energetic matrix** of the physical body. This "**Ether duplicate**" or "**double**" of the physical body is a subtle body of energetic vitality that evenly doubles the form of the physical body. The ether body feeds the physical body by vital energy. Without the ether body, the physical body cannot exist. Moreover, the ether body may be considered as a model from which the physical body is constructed. The ether body, like the physical body, has each of our vital organs in an energetic form interacting with the physical organs to help keep them healthy. If any physical organ or extremities are lost, their ethereal counterparts do not change and still exist; the ether body remains whole.

All degrees and kinds of an ether material are included into the structure of the ether "double" in different proportions. The proportions are determined by many factors, including characteristics such as race, ethnicity, type, and individual karma. Ether material of different densities is composed of different compound parts, which in turn form compounds of chemical elements.

The ether body rises up to two inches over the human physical body, penetrating it as well. An experienced clairvoyant with developed higher vision (vision of three, five or four-dimensional worlds) is able to perceive the difference between physical material and energy on the ether level. The study of ethereal vibrations and changes caused by higher vibrations and forces opens a wide field for exploration for researchers possessing higher vision or methods for their observation.

C.W. Leadbeater, performed a great deal of study and research on "man visible and invisible." Leadbeater revealed how a human may be seen from the other subtle bodies' points of view. He emphasized an ability to observe not only physical forms of radiation, but also the **ether "double,"** which is of almost the same size as the physical body. Vital energy penetrates the ether "double," and vital "world fluids" absorbed and assimilated by the organism, which circulate as light pink electric currents inside the body. Sometimes they are seen as luminous flows outside of healthy people. Ether "double" and nerve fluids are dense enough in reality, and although they are not seen by normal sight, they belong not only to the ether world but to the physical world as well.

Bio-energetic healing occurs on the ether level. During a life span, the ether body builds and restores the health of the physical body. In turn, the ether body demands energy healing, cleansing, balancing and normalizing in order to be healthy. A healthy ether body differs depending on the accumulation of vital energy, which passes through the solid body and influences its physical organs positively. All other subtle bodies acquire energy from the ether body. A developed and healthy ether body makes an individual hardy and able to work "energetically" and effectively. People with healthy and balanced ether bodies rarely become ill.

Signs of a highly developed ether body are great physical health, hardiness, flexibility, physical strength, and a powerful inner potential.

Astral Body

The astral body is connected with the physical body during its normal waking state. It is separated by death or a deep sleep. The astral body is represented by an egg-form cloudy mass containing a core of even more dense "material and energy" in the middle. This core has the size and shape of the physical body. The egg-form surrounding the core is called the "**astral aura**," which extends out from people up to 1.5 feet.

The astral body (the body of desires) possesses extraordinary mobility, and depending on the emotional state, it can manifest different shapes and sizes at once. When professionally trained, an individual may move instantaneously in the astral body in the area of the moon gravitational field (out-of-body experience) with an unbelievable speed. The astral body belongs to the astral world. Clairvoyants possess an ability to travel in the astral plane. They perceive with astral vision. For clairvoyants, it is easy to observe things located thousands of miles away as well as things that are before them. Aspects of space and time belong only to the physical world; they are absent outside the physical world. If a clairvoyant wishes to perceive any thing or assess an energy state of any body, they can be transited to that object via their astral body and observe it from all sides.

All things in the astral world may have an absolutely different and more comprehensive appearance than when viewed in the physical world. According to Leadbeater, in the astral plane, things may be seen from all sides at once. Moreover, they may be seen from the inside as well as from the outside. A clairvoyant with a developed astral vision can perceive any object from all sides, inside and outside, at once. There is no perspective on the astral plane, and all subjects or sides are equal.

When the astral vision is highly developed, a clairvoyant perceives physical material from the astral plane, and he or she may increase its microscopic particles to see better. For a such person, it is not difficult to see even ultraviolet and infrared waves, which are beyond the visible specter. An experienced clairvoyant will see the entire volume of the subject, distinguish vibrations of physical particles, and observe the astral "double" with its movements and vital energy flowing and glowing inside. He or she will also perceive the astral aura, which is less developed and complicated than the human aura. Finally, the true clairvoyant will also perceive the original essence, which penetrates the subject, moves instantaneously, and maintains the balance.

Upon studying auras of animals and humans, a clairvoyant perceives complicated energy systems by the same scheme, but performs a more complicated assessment for a more complicated system. Thereafter, because of the ability to transfer consciousness without any interruption, a real clairvoyant can remember on the physical plane all he or she studied or did on the other planes. An inexperienced "traveler" cannot understand what he or she "sees" in the astral world, and cannot explain it with "physical world" words, for it is not enough to see properly with astral vision in order to clearly decode astral information on the physical plane. This is why clairvoyants are trained to transfer their consciousness from one plane to another without any interruption in time. When this ability is developed, a clairvoyant may use astral abilities not only during sleep or trance when he or she is freed of the physical body, but during his or her awakening while still fully possessing the physical organs.

In deep sleep, higher parts of the human being combine with the astral body, gradually move out the physical body in a constant order, and stay close to the physical body. This is why we can see us traveling or standing on the side in our dreams. If a person is not thoroughly developed spiritually, his or her higher parts and astral body are in the same sleeping condition as the physical body, and the possibility to see dreams is highly decreased. Sometimes this person's astral body, being in a half-unconscious condition, travels by will of an astral stream, and meets either unusually pleasurable or unpleasant adventures on the way. After awakening, he or she remembers little, or from the sensual astral perception only, whereas persons with developed astral abilities may observe reality surrounding them in dreams and perceive many interesting and useful things in that reality. In this way, they use their astral abilities to perceive the complicated environment of astral reality. When trained to perceive astral reality fully in dreams, a person may utilize his sleeping time effectively and usefully without hindering the restful state the physical body needs for regeneration.

Observed from the astral plane, a human is seen as a luminous cloud of unusually complicated structure due to its oval form, sometimes called "an aural egg." Nevertheless, a clairvoyant may perceive organs and fluids inside the human, in addition to the aura outside the human. A more glowing aura is more easily seen, though it consists of the more subtle (astral) material and energy, which constantly change in color vibrations, depending on the constantly changing emotions and wishes in the human consciousness. This is the aura of the astral body. The human aura is often seen as an astral subject. The glowing, colored radiance of the astral aura often attracts clairvoyants by its appearance.

The astral body is the first subtle body that is extended over the physical body. This body and all higher bodies share the same place in space: a more subtle body penetrates a more dense body. Thus, a newly trained clairvoyant cannot distinguish one from another at a first glance; perception requires continuous study and extensive practice.

Studying the body of a newborn, a sensitive individual may find an astral material and energy of different density, and also ether material of different heaviness. When clearing the roots of these internal human bodies, it can be understood that agents of God's Karma form an ether "double," which may be considered as the matrix for the creation of the physical body. At the same time, astral material is formed in the astral plane by an unconscious automatic way of our ego in its descent to the material.

Physical manifestations of the astral body include vivacity, activity, vitality, cheerfulness, laughter, and the ability to feel joy. A highly developed astral body results in the ability to deeply identify with an image of an another individual besides one's self, actor's mastery, and inspiration.

Mental Body

The next body is **the mental body** (the body of thoughts). It consists of even more subtle material and energy than the astral body, which correlate to forms of the mental plane. Nevertheless, the mental body has the same structure as the astral body, and it also consists of a core and mental aura.

In its nature and purpose, the mental body is more complicated than the astral body. Colors of a person's mental body with its aura vary from one person to the next, reflecting the person's general orientation and personality. A person retains these colors throughout his or her life if he or she maintains health.

Actually, in the normal waking state a human "aural egg" in its middle has four of the same sized contours of a human form penetrating each other - the physical, ethereal, astral, and mental forms, and around them their auras. Usually, we can see our physical body with only our physical sight, our astral body with only our astral sight, our mental body with only the mental vision, and so on.

However, a clairvoyant who has practiced for many years can distinguish ether, astral, and mental auras or different parts of the whole "aural egg" not totally, but separately. Even so, it is not necessary to distinguish subtle energetic bodies to effectively perform bio-energy healing, and you will later see how it can be performed using our method.

The mental body (mind, intellect) connects to the physical body by Chinese meridians (**chi**) or Indian **nadis**. Nadis act as channels carrying vital energy from one subtle body to another. The mental body has a determined volume along with extension in time. When the mental body is highly developed, it appears as perfect and delightful in the clairvoyant's eyes.

A true purpose of our existence is cultivating spiritual life. An undergrowth of development will be dangerous for those who neglect to achieve astral and mental consciousness. There are people with the karmic potential to develop higher mental abilities. Nevertheless, this progress must be gradual, and not without passing through the astral development.

Clairvoyants who have perfectly developed their astral vision cannot entirely observe the mental body; nevertheless, they may freely move from the astral to the mental plane and use the higher possibility and subtle distinctness of the mental plane. Working on the mental plane, extra-sensitive people construct a temporary "artificial" astral body. Such a body, a copy of a human look, does not contain its own astral body material, and it is the same thing as "materialization" for the physical body.

We use the mental body in our actions, behaviors, and thoughts. The mental body is the strongest body of an individual, whereas the peak of a soul is the body of Nirvana.

Signs of a highly developed mental body are mental creativity, hardiness in mental work, the quantity and total volume of knowledge, logic, logic memory, velocity of the thought process, an eagerness to philosophic and scientific knowledge, the absence of emotions in the thought process, and self-control.

Karmic Body

Next, high and beautiful, **the karmic** or **causal body** is extended, almost covering the body. The karmic body is presented by an image of vital light and is the implement of the outer **ego**, or "**I**." It shows the boundary to which our actual "I" has risen through all past lives. The karmic body is the ruler of our ego.

Before transforming to the karmic level, our ego exists at a high level of the mental body, its real place of existence. Then, on the karmic level, our ego is controlled and expressed to the outer world at the first time. The karmic body becomes the only "engine" for our ego.

To materialize on lower planes or to return to the material or lower sides of the inner-self, our ego descends to the lower plane of the mental body or to another surrounding, keeping fully its karmic body and attracting these planes or surroundings to the karmic body. Our ego constructs its own mental body in these planes or surroundings to exist in this new environment. It forms its own astral body by the same way as the mental body. At the end of the descent to the material-self, our ego reaches our ether and physical bodies, or the lower planes. Thereafter, our ego's physical body is formed in the middle of the "aural egg," which represents a whole human.

Construction of the physical body itself is a very complicated process, and it presupposes an endless multitude of compounds. Nevertheless, karma agents construct a model, an energetic image of the physical body (**the matrix**) from which the physical body will be constructed.

The karmic body rules all functions of a cosmic organism (a living thing). This is one of the important qualities of the karmic body. All reasons of all events occur in the lower planes, and all unconscious traits of past lives determining an individual's present being and destiny are kept in the karmic body. Development of the karmic body creates the possibility to take a look at previous lives and control ego in the future. Psychic strength, which an individual receives at birth, and a psychic's either altruistic or selfish direction is a consequence of all previous incarnations.

To see this highly complicated subtle body, a clairvoyant must be experienced in the discernment of the plane to which each of the higher bodies belongs. From the beginning of practice, it is necessary to maintain two things. First, these auras must not be considered as simple emanations but as a part of manifestations of our ego in different planes. Second, one must remember that the whole human structure is considered as an "aural egg," not only as a physical body, which occupies only a middle part of this "egg." These things will be helpful in avoiding many difficulties in the comprehension and assessment of subtle bodies.

The karmic body is more subtle and dynamic than the mental body. The karmic body plays a very important and cardinal role among other bodies. Strength of the karmic body is connected to the knowledge of an individual and fulfillment of the primary Law of karmic development, or all terms and laws of structures, in which we act as small parts.

Perfect development in the karmic plan controls over thoughts and emotions, and helps to maintain psychic health. Signs of a highly developed karmic body are perfect attention, economy of the strengths, time, fulfillment of duty, concentration, unselfishness, realization, and observance of norms in human behavior.

Intuitive Body

The next body is the **intuitive body** (intuition, superconsciousness). The intuitive body is developed more or less in almost all people. For example, many people have experienced moments when intuition gave out the most intelligent decision at once in the most unexpected times; the intuitive body is powerful. Besides controlling visions of the past, the intuitive body may predict the future. Signs of a highly developed intuitive body are love of harmony and beauty, an intuitive feeling of consonance and dissonance, knowledge of the world's laws of harmony, ability to visualize images, perfect sight and hearing memory, the ability to enter into dreams, and development of spirit sight (the third eye).

Nirvana Body

The Nirvana body is an alliance of our ego and the Universe, as well as union with Truth and Love. If ego represents the love of the self, love in the Nirvana body is characterized by loving everything outside ego. Signs of a developed Nirvana body are spirit cleanliness, trust, kindness, compassion, ability to live for others, faith, and truth.

Absolute Body

The last outer body - **the Absolute body** - is a consequence of the development of all bodies of a cosmic organism, the harmonic unity of all best qualities and all kinds of development. If expectation of a human life is an improvement of a karmic matter, so the Absolute body regulates human behavior in according to expectations of life.

Reincarnation

In philosophy, a universal life can be viewed as the connection of two beginnings - spiritual and material. The link that puts these aspects together is the consciousness, which in turn unites two other categories: life and death. The light of consciousness is life, whereas rupture of consciousness is death. Ancient philosophers had seen the meaning of life in the expanding **Light of Consciousness**, achievement of Absolute Consciousness, which does not break after the physical body's death leading to eternity.

After physical death, humans have different ways of extending their existence into the spheres of the Absolute World, and not always with human faces. Philosophers have always been interested in the topics of Eternal Life and Instant Reincarnation. It is thought that as a physical body, subtle bodies are exposed to processes of decomposing and death. Many religions have practiced elaborate rituals of burial and commemoration according to terms of the dropping of different subtle bodies. Three days after the physical body's death, an energetic covering containing energetic information - the subtle body's essence - leaves the ether body, which comes to ruin. After nine days the astral body's essence leaves its body, after 40 days - the mental body's essence, after 114 days - the karmic body's essence, and after 146 days - the intuitive body's essence. After 666 days, Nirvana's essence may penetrate into Absolute (white if the Nirvana body is developed, or black if it is not developed or an anti-nirvana body is developed as well).

A mirrored reflection of Nirvana exists where the feeling of love leading to creation is substituted with the feeling of hatred leading to destruction. This anti-world is associated with the Shiva world in the Hinduism and the Lucifer world in Christianity. If an anti-nirvana body was developed by an individual in life, the essence will penetrate the Black Absolute.

The ether body belonging to an individual's physical body is decomposed after death, whereas all other subtle bodies are saved for prospective evolutionary development. One life in one physical body is not enough for the subtle body to develop completely. Every human passes through an individualized chain of evolutionary development. Researchers in the reincarnation field state that every human can live many lives; however, humans do not realize themselves after death, and when they are born again, they lose their past memories. Nevertheless, when alive, an individual has achieved the highest cosmic development, so he or she has a possibility to remember the past life. Using special techniques, an individual is able to review past lives, including forgotten experiences and knowledge. The most important precedent for this is the quality of past lives. Aspiration toward the white Absolute and endeavoring to develop the cosmic organism (the whole self) gives the possibility for transition to the other more complicated spheres of universal subtle worlds in a relatively short term - perhaps a few tens of lives.

Universe's Properties

Everything in the universe, from God to a grain of sand, is the manifestation of a Sole Substance named **Akasha** (quintessence, or fifth element). Akasha is associated with hearing in the physical organism. Akasha is the primary and basic material from which all in the world is formed, including humans; it is the bridge between being and nonbeing. Everything is concluded in Akasha: subtle "invisible" occurrences are represented in the aspect of vibration, whereas the solid or "visible" by human sight is represented in the aspect of physical matter.

The universe is filled with a subtle, vital force named **Prana**. There is an instant and constant flow of this cosmic energy into humans. Without Prana activity, Akasha stays as a shapeless and lifeless dark space.

We cannot see Prana, but we can see its manifestations. Electricity is one way to observe Prana's manifestation. Prana is a vital force, like a gas of great power, penetrating everywhere, coming from the Great Unknown. Prana submits to human consciousness and follows thought and mental control. Prana can be both creative and destructive energy. As healthful energy, Prana possesses tremendous strength and is necessary for our well-being bringing vitality. If blood has little Prana, illness will occur.

Intelligent work with Prana promotes spiritual growth, prosperity and vitality in our lives. Yogis determine Prana flow as healing energy. If one is aware that Prana submits mental direction or thought energy, one can utilize enormous amounts of the vital energy using visualization and meditation. An individual trained and able to direct Prana abundance around ill people becomes a healer. The warmth of Prana energy radiating from a healer's hands is a real sign of his or her ability to heal.

Categories of Polarities

Chemical elements that enter our physical bodies via food products cause **negative polarity** (-) in our vital strength. These elements can be solid, fluid, or gaseous elements of nature matter. The Earth is a giant reservoir of negative polarity. Negative elements and chemical compounds enter into the human bloodstream and into the heart. The heart, working as a pump, delivers them into the lungs, where they unite with Prana, the solar energy of **positive polarity** (+). These positive-negative forces penetrate the blood as dew penetrates the earth. These vital forces belong to the ether body, whereas oxygen belongs to the physical body. In this way, positive-negative forces enter the organism and charge every cell by vital energy.

The polarity of positive and negative (Chinese symbols are **yang** and **yin**) is a balancing force between all forms of energy and matter, and it is a necessity for every structure to exist. Foods also have polarities. Everything in the cosmos is characterized by positive, negative, or neutral energy. We cannot identify positive and negative as good and bad in the physical bodies; both these kinds of energy are necessary to maintain life and the vital flow of energies.

When the human physical body sleeps, positive-negative forces regenerate damaged cells. This process is as natural as any of the body's functions: transforming food energy into vital energy, regenerating blood cells in red marrow, the regulating of heart pulsation and breathing and so on.

Breathing, which seems so simple, is controlled by a cycle of electromagnetic impulses passing from the medulla oblongata (a pyramidal ending part of the spinal cord in the neck area, united with the spinal column) down to the solar plexus, where the lungs expand and contract. That force, which transmits electric and magnetic impulses to the diaphragm's muscle on the ether level, is determined as Prana. On the physical level, all processes in the body are controlled by electrical impulses between cells with the help of chemical reactions.

An even flow of positive-negative current brings a sedating effect on the nervous system; the nervous system regenerates itself when Prana flows freely. Constancy of the ether flow balances vital energy for the organisms. The human body may be compared with a giant atom-illness occurs when positive-negative polarities are not balanced. In the same way, the relationship of this giant atom and its energetic covering occurs as a union of polarities.

Polarity not only affects all processes in the physical body, but also relationships between physical bodies and subtle bodies and between the universe and humans. Physical bodies and subtle bodies are kept close by the polarity of positive-negative. All bodies interact with each other because of their differences in densities of energy fields. Physical bodies are consist of the densest, or slowest energy and are considered negative, whereas subtle bodies, in order of descent from the physical body, become more complex and faster in energy, and are considered positive. Polarities interacting between all these bodies must stay in balance all the time. Thus, an imbalance flowing from the highest energy fields to the lower brings illnesses on the physical level. Bringing energy in without the cleansing of energies may cause even more imbalance. Nevertheless, any energetic movement may also be directed in the reverse way in order to achieve the balance between the energies again. Later you will learn a unique method of cleansing and balancing the bio-energy fields.

The Balance of Body/Emotion/Mind/Soul

When we determine **the balance of body/emotion/mind/ soul**, we are referring to the balance of polarities in each aspect. The body is a negative pole, emotion and soul are neutral, and the mind is a positive pole. On the physical level, an energetic imbalance can occur because of improper foods or poor diet, bringing an acid/ alkaline imbalance and toxins into the body. On the emotional level, unbalanced emotions bring negativity instead of peace (the neutral state). Lack of soul purity and spirituality are imbalances on the soul (Nirvana) and intuitive levels. Finally, negative or pessimistic thoughts bring a negative, rather than positive, mental orientation.

An acid/alkaline imbalance, toxins, unbalanced emotions or negative thought patterns affect the harmony of the **whole bio-energy system**. Patterns of negative energy cause abnormalities to all normal processes in the physical bodies. If negative, harmful energy and abnormal processes continue to exist, they finally destroy the physical body. This is why people need to heal any imbalances in their bio-energy systems.

Bio-Positive Energy vs. Bio-Negative Energy

Bio-energy can be explained as bio-electromagnetic energy. When we use the term "**bio-positive energy**," we mean the pure healing energy coming from God when positive energy flows freely in energy systems, bringing vitality and health. Without bio-positive energy, there is no life. **Bio-negative energy**, however, is trapped, disharmonious, stale, or stagnant energy that blocks pathways and prevents vital energy from freely flowing in the energy systems.

Negative energy brings imbalances into energetic systems and causes illnesses and emotional trauma.

Bio-energy healing and balancing involves cleansing the energy system of bio-negative energy, allowing bio-positive energy to flow freely in the system in order to restore energetic balance and health. With energy balancing, you will be able to heal physical problems in the physical bodies as well as imbalances on the energetic level. In bio-energetics, any illness is perceived as an energy imbalance. When the energy is balanced, this influences the physical body positively.

Bio-positive energy is an essential element in maintaining physical, psychic and energetic health. However, in current practices, healers often do not pay attention to the directions of movements, aspects of bio-positive and bio-negative energy, and the withdrawal of weak energy. Weak and stale energy must be relieved in order to let vital energy flow in and out of a freely balancing energy system.

Later you will be able to correct physical problems and illnesses using methods of energy cleansing, balancing, normalizing, and healing.

Chapter Two

Chakras as Psychic and Energetic Centers

Every subtle body communicates to the others and the universe through psychic centers. The universe is composed of spinning wheels and spirals of energy. Any organism gathers cosmic energy through nonphysical vortices of pure energy-energetic "transformers" named **chakras** (See Figure 1). According to ancient tradition, psychic centers located in the ether body have the energetic forms of lotuses. In the physical body, chakras are represented in the forms of plexuses and endocrine glands.

Chakras are an essential part of our bio-energy system, being its energetic centers. All humans have and use their chakras, even if they are not aware of them. In Sanskrit, the chakra is a wheel of life, an energetic circuit. Chakras enable us to gather energy from the cosmos, process it, use it, and even release it back. Gathered cosmic energy can be kept in the subtle bodies, and when needed can be transformed by chakras to the physical body for its proper functioning (this process is reversible as well).

The chakra system is an active, self-perpetuating spiral. Each chakra, as a spinning antenna, receives and filters energy from cosmos and delivers it to a particular physical organ in its area or endocrine gland, supplementing them with prana energy. Much of the chakras work is concerned not only with specific areas of the body, but also with the maintenance of a healthy balance between the individual's subtle bodies and the physical body and different

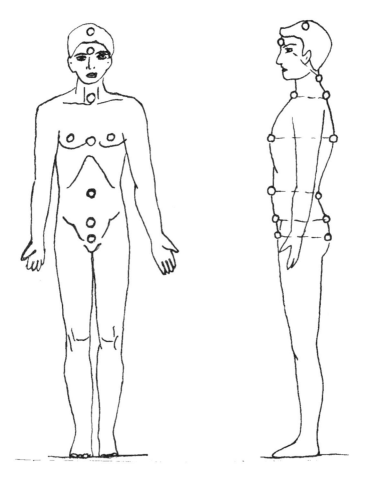

Figure 1. Chakras

areas in the whole bio-energetic system.

Chakras are interdependent and interconnected centers of the chakra system. Chakras influence each other in their work. If one chakra is unbalanced and not working properly, it affects others and leads to a general imbalance of the chakra system. A healthy, active chakra increases the energetic potential of all chakras, whereas an unbalanced and dysfunctional chakra decreases normal energy flow in the chakra system and slows down the whole organism and the entire energy system. Even one dysfunctional chakra in the chakra system causes more chakras to close. This dysfunction leads to an occurrence of energetic imbalances, physical illnesses, and emotional blocks in the energy system.

Ancient Indian thought determined the nonphysical energetic centers as sites of consciousness. The chakras' tops are represented as plexuses or brains of the nervous system. From this point of view, the chakra system may be accepted as a model of consciousness. The consciousness of all living organisms is based on energy traveling through the energetic systems. Chakras are centers of different levels of consciousness, ranging from the "base" level to the high spiritual.

The major chakras are located on the spinal column and on the head, and one chakra is located in the heart plexus. Every physical organ has a minor chakra, and there are many minor or secondary chakras around the human body. All acupuncture points are chakras as well. Many authors believe that minerals have one chakra, while animals have three or four. Humans have seven major in-body chakras, one minor chakra, and one very important out-of-body chakra. We believe that more out-of-body chakras will be discovered in the not-too-distant future.

Next, let's review what you need to know about human chakras to perform chakra healing (See Figure 2).

Muladhara (Root Chakra)

The first chakra is **Muladhara**, located at the base of the spine. Energy wave fluctuations of this base chakra correspond to the color red. Red has the lowest vibration rate in the visible spectrum, thus it affects the most dense or material matter in our organisms. Muladhara affects and is most affected by the physical body.

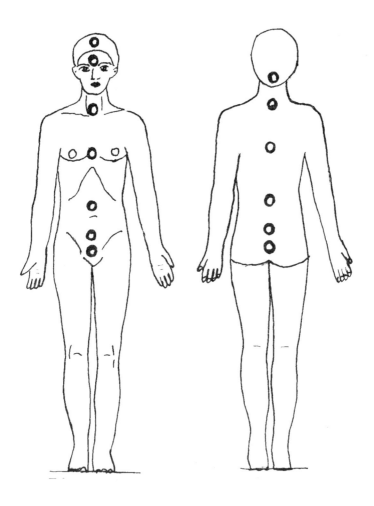

Figure 2. Chakras on the Front and Back

Nevertheless, it gives an awareness of eternal life and the divinity of individuals. Many researchers think that this chakra of the physical plane belongs to the ether body. **The root chakra** plays a connecting role between the center of physical energy (Ajna chakra) and the center of psychic energy (Sahasrara chakra). The Muladhara chakra is responsible for the normal condition of the five senses, sex, and physical growth. The root chakra is associated with survival, stability, structure, manifestation, and patience.

Svadhisthana (Sacral Chakra)

The second chakra is named **Svadhisthana** and is located in the sacrum (lower abdomen). Energy wave fluctuations correspond to the color orange. **The sacral chakra** corresponds to the ether body. Many researchers think that the chakra of the physical plane (Muladhara), along with Svadhisthana, are comparable belongings of the ether body. Certainly, they are similar to each other by their energetic functions. Nevertheless, the sacral chakra is more complex than the root chakra. Muladhara absorbs electromagnetic fields from the earth (through the ground chakra) that are necessary for the physical body. Svadhisthana, which produces an internal energy, utilizes the prana of food matter, which it distributes along meridians to the organs of the physical body and to the other energetic centers and subtle bodies.

The sacral chakra controls our energetic states. The health of our physical bodies depends on this chakra's activity. As the entire ether body, the sacral chakra is important for our well-being and vitality, and is associated with abundance, pleasure, and the inspiration to create. Svadhisthana is responsible for prosperity, desire, sexuality, and accelerating the healing process. Interactions of Svadhisthana with other chakras determine the influence of food intake on our energetic manifestations (Manipura-chakra), sexuality (Muladhara-chakra), and emotional sphere (Anahata-chakra).

Manipura (Solar Plexus Chakra)

The third chakra is **Manipura**, located on the fifth lumbar (abdomen) vertebra. The chakra's energy corresponds to the energy of the color yellow. Manipura is related to the astral subtle body; through the solar plexus chakra, a connection between the chakra's system and astral body's energy and substance is kept.

The solar plexus chakra controls our emotional states, and emotions are directly linked with our sense of well-being and health. Manipura also accumulates and distributes energies which are produced in other chakras. Manipura governs personal power, self-worth, self-confidence, self-esteem, decision-making, metabolic energy, and insight.

Anahata (Heart Chakra)

The forth major chakra is **Anahata** (**the heart chakra**). It is located on the fifth thoracic vertebra (on the chest). Anahata's energy color is green. It relates to the mental body. The heart chakra is the beginning to higher consciousness and spirit, and it keeps the balance between the three lower chakras and the three upper chakras. Anahata chakra helps in the mastery of language and poetry. As the mental body, its chakra determines mental creativity, logic, memory, velocity of the thought process, eagerness to philosophical and scientific knowledge, and self-control. It brings a balance of action and joy and promotes wisdom, intelligence, and inner strength. Anahata chakra affects our actions, behaviors, and thoughts, and keeps the balance within the physical body.

Vishuddha (Throat Chakra)

The fifth chakra is **Vishuddha**, located on the first thoracic vertebra on the thyroid level (throat). The energy color is blue. This chakra connects to the karmic body. **The throat chakra** brings knowledge, creativity, communication ability, purity, calmness, and mastery of the individual's entire self. At this level, an individual expresses the entire self and his or her ego verbally, and shows the inner-self to the outer world. Here, emotions may be expressed in forms such as painting, singing, or writing. The throat chakra controls and expresses both thoughts and emotions.

The throat chakra gives energy to the voice and desire to express the individual self. Voice power shows the throat chakra's strength, whereas a weak voice shows the throat chakra's imbalance. Differences in the voice reflect the state of the moment: emotions, sexual arousal, love, or a thought state. It brightly shows the interconnection between chakras.

Ajna (Third Eye)

The sixth chakra is named **Ajna (the third eye chakra)**. It is located on the second cervical vertebra (on the neck), and on the forehead between the eyebrows (on the front, or medula plexus). The forehead location is called **the Third Eye**, and it is connected to the intuitive body. The energy color is dark blue (indigo). Ajna is the center of physical energy, and the transformer of universal energy or energetic information to the physical body and to other chakras as well. Through the third eye chakra, a universal energy is channeled to the physical body. The chakra governs growth and coordination on the physical level, and it allows mastery in spiritual and emotional growth as well.

Moreover, through Ajna chakra, we are able to open ourselves to the universal creative energy, or energetic information. The Ajna chakra perceives energetic information and commands where the information should proceed in the system. The Third Eye is a source of superconsciousness (the unconscious sphere of consciousness), spiritual wisdom, clairvoyance, imagination, and intuitive insight. With a developed third eye, we may become perceivers of past, present, and future. The Third Eye is a place where the balance between mind, emotions, spirituality, and the physical body may be achieved in order to create, heal, and perceive universal and divine information. We may achieve and control our balance and awareness in a state of enlightenment; this is why thought can be creative and healing. Thus, through our imagination, wisdom, and creative abilities, we can lead ourselves to healthy, happy, and fulfilling lives.

Openness to spirituality may significantly change our understanding of our inner selves and our connections with an outer world and other people. Through the third eye chakra, we may transform ourselves into spiritual beings and control our minds as spiritual masters do. The healthy chakra, with its highly developed intuition, leads to overall well-being and happiness.

Through the Ajna chakra, one reveals the divine within the self and reflects divinity within others. An opened and functional Third Eye chakra dissipates ego, duality and reveals the sense of oneness with the Universe and unity with the cosmic laws. Intuition, inner vision, insight, divine wisdom, spiritual and emotional growth come into reality in the Third Eye chakra. At the Ajna level, one may express theories, ideas, and ideologies.

Central

The chakra of the Nirvana body is the **Central**, located on the heart plexus. The energy color is violet. The Central chakra is a link between our physical bodies and Nirvana (the world of Love) body through our hearts. Waves of violet color have the highest vibration rate in the color spectrum. Unconditional love, brother's love, universal love, and true love begin in this chakra. People with open hearts show compassion, forgiveness, and desire for genuine love and affection.

Sahasrara (Crown Chakra)

The seventh major chakra is **Sahasrara**, located on the top of the head. The color is white. Through Sahasrara chakra, we receive universal cosmic energy and energetic information from God or the Divine Center. Sahasrara represents the highest aspect of the Self as a cosmic organism. It is linked to the Absolute body (the conclusion of the development of all seven subtle bodies of a cosmic organism), and it relates to the whole being. Sahasrara chakra is a center of psychic energy. The **crown chakra** is the most purified and evolved energy level in the bio-energy system, a balanced and perfected universal wisdom.

The goal of a human is to improve one's own karma by living a "good" life, and a healthy Sahasrara chakra regulates human behavior and personal characteristics to live a life in accordance with karmic law. Sahasrara chakra is a center of spirituality, refinement, and magnificence. Through the crown chakra, human spirit connects to Universal Spirit, and the spiritual being moves toward Universal Consciousness-the individual self is fully dissolved here. At the crown chakra level, the cosmic self opens to the Source, unites with cosmic principles, and governs the entire universe within the body. The crown chakra is associated with universal knowledge and spiritual understanding, and is the only chakra that follows the subtle body in cosmic spheres after death.

The Ground Chakra

If the crown chakra connects one with the cosmos and the Divine Source, **the ground chakra** connects one with the Earth. People need to be grounded, for they belong to the earth in order to fulfill their lives, abilities, and experiences. Even as one becomes highly developed in spiritual growth, healing, intuitive or extrasensory perception, one must stay grounded and centered. An ungrounded individual is not able to cope with everyday problems, stress or feelings, and may be unfocused, as if he or she is out of the body. The ground chakra (located lower than human feet, out of the human body) lets us throw out waste (used) energy from all chakras and subtle bodies in a natural way.

Nadis and Sushumna

Chakras are activated by prana energy (**White Light**), and they control this life-force as it enters the human organism. Transformed by each chakra, the vital energy flows through **meridians** (acupuncture channels) or **nadis** (channels or energetic streams). Nadis link with chakras.

The sum total of the chakras forms a vertical column in our bodies called **sushumna** (central channel). Two other major nadis that function with sushumna are **ida** and **pingala**. They start in the same place as sushumna, and, when energized, they begin to move in spiral fashion in opposite directions up along sushumna, each pacing the other. The ida is a left channel. It is lunar, feminine. The pingala is a right channel-solar, masculine. In Indian tradition, ida and pingala meet the sushumna in the third eye and then separate: the ida exits through the left nostril, and the pingala exits through the right nostril.

These major nadis are activated when **Kundalini energy** (creative Absolute energy) is aroused from its seat. A harmonic combination of all the best qualities and highly developed subtle bodies gives **Kundalini-Shakti** a possibility to ascend through all chakras to her white fraction in Sahasrara chakra. It also allows reception of information from the Universe (the Absolute World) and spiritual travel in it as well. For awakening and traveling Kundalini, which can be compared to fire, it is necessary that all chakras and subtle bodies be highly developed, cleansed, balanced, normalized, and healed.

Chakras' Performance

The human organism, its functioning, and the condition of its subtle bodies depends on the chakras' work, or spinning. When the chakras are spinning effectively, they bring balanced functioning to the organism, a free-flowing of energies, and harmony between consciousness and subconsciousness and between inner and outer worlds as well.

Chakras show patterns of electromagnetic activity. When all chakras work properly (spinning not too slow or too fast), a physical organism is in perfect health and powerful energetic shape. When the chakra is opened and functional, it can perform its work perfectly, process prana energy, bring energy to the physical organs and subtle bodies, and remove used stale or stagnant energy from the system.

When the chakra is closed or blocked, it stops spinning and becomes dysfunctional. Chakras may become closed when they are congested with stale or stagnant energy. One way they can close is during an instance of fight-or-flight response of the organism. This response is a natural way for the organism to become alert and prepared to any danger or unusual situation. However, if this stressful condition of the body is left uncontrolled and continues for a long time, the chakras may stay closed and dysfunctional. When the physical body stays in prolonged stress (distress) or depression, the chakras cannot spin and work properly; they become unbalanced, blocked with stale and stagnant energy and unbalanced.

Our thoughts and attitudes can block energy flowing through the chakras as well. Unexpressed emotions can cause the chakras to be overcharged, leading to their closing or blockage. Personality problems both cause and are caused by energy imbalances. Imbalances in the chakra system of the physical body reveal themselves through both negative personality and physical illness: dysfunctional chakras cause imbalances in the subtle energetic bodies, and imbalances in the subtle bodies then manifest in personal, psychological and emotional problems.

When chakras are closed, energy cannot be transformed and released to the physical body. If energy is not flowing freely through energetic systems, physical problems may develop in specific areas, and discomfort or illness can occur in the organism. When a chakra is blocked, it needs healing by uncovering and removing whatever is blocking it. The clearing of congested energy from the human energy system becomes a necessary prophylactic way for keeping the organism healthy.

Because the chakras work together as a system, a block in the functioning of one chakra may affect the activity of another. These chakras are especially inter-related: (a) the root chakra and the third eye tie, (b) the sacral chakra and throat chakra, and (c) the solar plexus chakra and heart chakra. If one chakra is not functioning, it must be cleansed, balanced, normalized, and healed together with the associate chakra accordingly.

Chakras are interrelated not only with parasympathetic and sympathetic autonomous nervous systems, but endocrine systems as well. Chakras transform vital energy to the endocrine glands. The root chakra (Muladhara) correlates to the testicles, the sacral chakra (Svadhisthana) - the ovaries, the solar plexus chakra (Manipura) - the adrenals and pancreas, the heart chakra (Anahata) - the thymus, the throat chakra (Vishuddha) - the thyroid and parathyroid, the third eye chakra (Ajna) - the pineal gland, and the crown chakra (Sahasrara) - the pituitary (master) gland.

Chakras feed the life-force into our endocrine systems, which regulates our hormonal balance.

During our many years as healers, we have observed that healthy chakras spin in a clockwise direction in a front of a body (Figure 3) and in the same way in both sexes, whereas closed, unbalanced chakras spin in a counterclockwise direction, stay still, spin in eclipses or move unevenly. The energy balance of the bio-energy system, which is very important to our general well-being and health, can be achieved by energy that is in a constant smooth flow, refreshed and vitalized, aided by constantly spinning chakras.

Characteristics Brought by Opened and Closed Chakras

The Root Chakra

When the root chakra is open and functional, it provides vital energy, stability, survival, solid structure, security, patience, and manifestation.

When closed, it causes fear, frustration, lack of fulfillment, restlessness, and a feeling of disconnection. Energy deficiency or depleted energy through a closed or blocked first chakra causes terminal illnesses, and vice versa.

The Sacral Chakra

When the sacral chakra is open and functional, it provides a good appetite, genteel taste, desire, pleasure, vitality, pride, emotion, sexual satisfaction, and prosperity.

When closed, it causes greed, manipulation, sentimentality, exhaustion, and guilt.

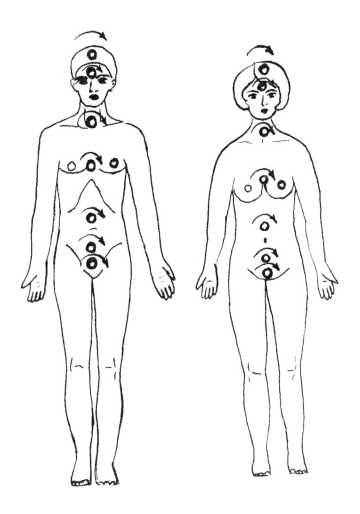

Figure 3. Chakras' Natural Spinning

The Solar Plexus Chakra

When this chakra is opened and functional, people are able to make decisions and understand personal power and the inner-self. A working solar plexus chakra brings nourishment, balance, intelligence, personal power, self-confidence, and self-respect.

When the chakra is closed, it causes unworthiness, fear of failure, inability to make decisions, lack of confidence, low self-respect, apathy, and inflexibility.

The Heart Chakra

An opened heart chakra means the beginning of higher consciousness and light. It brings a strong feeling of acceptance, empathy and joy. It shows individuality, unity, adaptability, generosity, purity, innocence, gentleness, dignity, and nobility.

The closed chakra may cause abhorrence, avarice, selfishness, meanness, malice, and anger.

The Throat Chakra

When the throat chakra is opened and functional, it shows willpower, creative visualization, skillful communication, orator mastery, artistry, spirituality, truthfulness, independence, and self-expression.

The throat chakra may become dysfunctional through blocks of emotional energy or suppressed anger and tears. The closed chakra may cause addictions, suppressed feelings, untruthfulness, dependency, lack of creativity and mastery, uncertain communication and gossip.

The Third Eye Chakra

When the third eye chakra is opened and functional, it brings spiritual perception, intuition, inner-sense, sense of unity with the universe, creative energy, an ability to bio-energy healing, and even telepathy and clairvoyance.

When the chakra is closed it causes iciness, pragmatism, meanness, mental tension, tightness, inability of spiritual perception, and tartness.

The Crown Chakra

When the crown chakra is developed, it leads to openness to the Divine Source, a feeling of unity with the universe, spirituality, faith, peace of inner-self, and enlightenment.

When it is not well-developed, the crown chakra causes hopelessness, depression, alcoholism, egoism, an inability to understand the inner-self, and disconnection with the spiritual world and Divine source.

Chapter Three

Meditation and Visualization - Preparing For Bio-Energetic Work

Development of Subtle Bodies

In order to grow spiritually, achieve deep understanding of your life purpose, maintain bio-energetic health, work with human energy, and help yourself and others, you need to improve your subtle bodies, especially the mental and intuitive bodies.

For your **ether body** development, we recommend the breathing exercises, Hatha yoga, and energy-gathering exercises in our book *Health by Bio-Energy and Mind*. Special methods for developing **the astral body** include bathing every day in cold water (water penetrates with astral energies), walking barefoot on grass, and meditation.

Characteristics of a highly developed **mental body** are mental creation, hardiness in mental work, quantity and total volume of knowledge, logic and image memories, velocity of thinking, desire of philosophic and scientific knowledge, abstinence of emotions in mental process, and self-control. In the process of knowledge accumulation and development of intellect, a feeling of mental superiority, and a haughty, agitated, and overstrained mind can become restraining factors. The freeing of these factors will increase the potential for developing the mental body.

The karmic body is more subtle and dynamic than the mental body. The karmic body is considered to be an important body that links to knowing our personality and obeying the dictates of universal karmic laws. In our lives, we should realize all terms of karmic laws, because we carry karma. Constant alleviation of bad habits and the meditative practicing of renunciating personal characteristics give good development in the karmic body.

Development of **the intuitive body** correlates to the development of intuition. Possessing the power of immediately understanding a task without conscious reasoning, study, or non-logical thinking is given to all humans. However, many people do not realize how important it is to develop intuitive power. With intuition, we are able to feel harmony or disharmony in any object, conception, or occurrence, and think of anything new. Characteristics of a highly developed intuitive body are love of harmony, an intuitive feeling of consonance and dissonance, knowledge of harmony laws of the world around, ability to visualize images, sharpness of visual and auditory memory, the ability to enter into dreams, and development of spiritual sight (the third eye).

To develop **the Nirvana body**, meditations focusing on dissolving the ego, focusing on the heart, and polishing such qualities as truthfulness, sincerity, nobility, and kindness are helpful.

It is necessary to mention that the total balancing of all subtle bodies is not needed, because such equilibrium of development prevents growth, progress, and a route to the high levels of development. A change of rhythms is required, giving the possibility of intentional break-up of the balance. An individual may choose one or two subtle bodies to develop in order of priority. The physical and the ether bodies must always be kept in health; you may choose to work from any of the others.

Preparing For Visualization

To develop understanding of our energetic being and energetic health and the ability to work with bio-energy (perceive and interpret energetic information), we will need to use our highly developed mental and intuitive bodies.

One of the most effective methods for developing the third eye and the intuitive body is **visualization**. An ability to visualize images at will and retain visual memory can be developed by practice. When you are relaxed, you may visualize color and hear correlating to its sound (the seven colors of the spectrum have seven musical notes correlating to these colors). Later, you may practice the visualization of color combination, seeing geometric or voluminous figures. A highly developed third eye leads to the ability to observe radiation of the subtle bodies or colored aura.

Visualization, like intuition, is a type of thinking which is used for making contact with the inner-self, rather than with the outer world. Employing images in our mental work to remember information precedes communication with words. Communicating with the inner-self using mental images requires our full attention to imagery.

Visualization means creating a mental picture or image as in your night dreams. These created images have the energy to influence you, and they can be animated by your mental energy. Mental images, being your energetic children, work for your well-being, bringing energetic and physical health. You, by managing energetic images, can help the healing process to occur. By visualizing the perfect consequence, your consciousness will be programmed to achieve it in reality.

For healing purposes, you should use **mental imagery**. Mental imagery is different from visualization in that it induces deep physical **relaxation** in addition to the process of visualization. The deeper the relaxation, the more vivid and controllable are the images, and the more they may be healing in their nature. Becoming relaxed, you may stimulate and facilitate vibrant mental healing images.

Relaxation of the physical body allows you to tune in to the inner-self, and mobilizes the bodies' resources for inward activity. The effects of relaxation include reduced heart rate, blood pressure, and sweating, increased functioning of the gastrointestinal tract, relaxation of muscles, and an increase of oxygen and blood flowing to the brain. One of the characteristics of the **relaxation response** is the rapid shifting of the brain-wave patterns from low-amplitude, rapid **beta waves** to higher-amplitude, slower, more strongly rhythmical **alpha** and **theta waves**. Beta waves occur mostly in the waking state, whereas alpha and theta waves are found in such states as meditation and contemplation.

The first and most important step in the process of visualization, mental imagery, or any energetic work is preparing the mind. As your physical body, your mind has to be calmed down, quieted, and eased into the special condition of the **alpha** and **theta state**.

The Meditative Mind State

Researchers have discovered that the human brain is powered by electricity. Brain waves or fluctuations of energy acting across the pathways of the brain can be registered by special devices, and even monitored on a display. In this way, an individual may see his or her present patterns of brain waves, which differ depending on the brain state. Scientists have found that the human brain has a tendency to produce brain waves of four frequencies, which they have termed **beta**, **alpha**, **theta**, and **delta**.

The most rapid waves are **beta waves**. Beta waves are present when we are in a "normal" state of mental arousal-walking, talking, and performing everyday tasks. These waves are dominant in our brains because of their association with alertness, arousal, concentration, and cognition. When beta waves are dominant, we keep our attention externally. When beta waves are present at excessive levels, they can bring anxiety.

The next most rapid waves are the **alpha waves**. Alpha waves appear in the brain when we close our eyes and relax our bodies. Bodily and mental passiveness or an unfocused state brings brain-wave activity down, causing the brain to produce dominant alpha waves, otherwise known as the **alpha state**. The alpha state is a neutral brain state, which can be achieved by people when they are without stress, are healthy and in a relaxed state. People with stress, mental or physical illness, or anxiety cannot achieve the alpha state because of a lack of alpha brain activity.

The next frequency, the **theta waves**, occur when calmness and relaxation deepen into drowsiness. The brain condition between waking and sleeping is called **theta state**. The very slow theta waves are often indicative of deep reverie, mental imagery, and the ability to access memories. In the theta state ("hypnagogic," or "twilight"), we are able to have daydreams or visualize unexpected dreamlike mental images, and have vivid memories, like of childhood or other pleasant memories. In the theta state, people can learn and memorize enormous amounts of a new information or new language quickly and effectively. Through theta activities, we can access our unconscious being, insight, and creative thoughts. In our active and busy times, adults produce the theta state rarely or not at all, whereas children are in the theta state almost all the time. It is the most mysterious state of the brain. However, it may be kept for any lengthy period of time only by experienced people because of the tendency to fall asleep when large amounts of theta waves are generated.

The slowest waves are **delta waves**, which the brain generates when falling asleep. When delta waves become the dominant brain waves, it means that we are either asleep or unconscious. Nevertheless, when our brains are in the **delta state**, they tend to release growth hormone.

Sitting with closed eyes in a relaxed, passive state, we may achieve the alpha and theta, or **meditative state**. In the beginning of practice, achieving the meditative state using EEG alpha-theta biofeedback may be helpful in learning to produce alpha and theta waves at will. Biofeedback is related to mind-body interaction. Using biofeedback, people can learn to manipulate their supposedly involuntary brain waves and generate large quantities of alpha waves. Biofeedback simply uses mechanical means to amplify certain internal cues and make people aware of them to gain the possibility of self-control.

Ideally, in achieving the meditative state, we should aspire to reach its peak. The meditative state of brain in its peak is characterized by the brain-wave activity throughout the whole brain (both left and right hemispheres). **Brain synchronization** is the state in which the two hemispheres of the brain become synchronized, both hemispheres generating the same brain waves. It is important to consider the relationship between the wave patterns of both hemispheres. When the brain hemispheres operate in synchronicity, the amplitude of the wave pattern throughout the entire cortex is powerfully increased (doubled). This represents forceful whole-brain fluctuations, resulting in the potential for brain reorganization at a higher order.

This peak state of brain synchrony, which may be experienced by experienced meditators, shows doubling waves increasing their efficiency. Experienced meditators are able to create the state of hemispheric synchronization. This state of whole-brain integration, with the same brain-wave frequencies throughout, is often accompanied by deep tranquility, flashes of creative insight, euphoria, intensely focused attention, and enhanced learning abilities.

How you can achieve the meditative state of mind that will be needed for your bio-energetic work? The ability to stay focused on a single thing may be achieved by frequent practice. *At first, choose a quiet place where nothing will disturb you. Relax your body, and release any tension from your body by tightening different groups of muscles for a moment, then relaxing them.*

Find a comfortable position for your body. To find the balance of your body, rock from side to side. Center yourself. **Centering** or **grounding** is an act of self-searching, understanding your inner-self and your relation to the universe. Through the centering, you may be aware of the dynamics of your own consciousness and the physical body. *Close your eyes.* Later, with more practice, you will be able to keep the eyes open and just diffuse your vision. *Achieve centering physically and psychologically, finding inside yourself reference or stability.* During the meditation, maintenance of a passive attitude will be helpful in achieving the meditative state.

Start to breathe with your abdomen slowly and quietly. In the beginning of your practice, pay attention to the **full abdominal breathing**. *With a deep exhalation, pull your abdomen in, whereas, with a deep inhalation, push the abdomen out.* With more practice, you will breathe deeply and automatically.

*Now add the chanting of a **mantra** (OM, KSHAM, HAM, YAM, RAM, VAM, LAM, or even "one") as a musical tone. Pronounce the mantra as you sing, "A-A-O-M-M-M..." Take a deep breath, then keep the exhalation going by pronouncing the mantra to increase the effect. Let the mantra find its own rhythm as you repeat it over and over again. Chant your mantra mentally* *or aloud,whichever way is more relaxing and comfortable to you.* All you do now is breath and chant the mantra; your consciousness is busy with chanting only. With this exercise, you develop the ability to focus your consciousness on the needed task or object. You may try counting, releasing tension in the body, or emptying your brain of thoughts as a subject of the meditation as well.

While you are relaxed, deeply breathing, and chanting, your brain starts generating alpha and theta waves. Now you are calm, intensely aware of both inner and outer realities, yet detached from both. Skilled meditators diffuse their vision and consciousness, becoming oneness with the universe. They have clear consciousness as long as they need it without the help of concentration on the object or any activity. For beginners, having a lot of thoughts and few moments of clear consciousness is normal; nevertheless, keep practicing to master gradually over the consciousness.

Meditation alone may be helpful in everyday life. During meditation you cannot worry, fear, or hate. Your body can learn to rid itself of anxiety, depression, hostility, or any stressful or habitual emotions. Nowadays, meditation is used in the prevention and healing of high blood pressure, heart problems, migraines, and arthritis.

To perform any bio-energetic work, which you will learn in later chapters, you will always need to enter into the meditative state of mind. Depending on what you are going do, you will need either to empty your mind of having any thoughts or **mental intention**.

Intention as Mental Command

The second step in preparing our minds for the visualization process and later, to bio-energetic healing, involves learning to give yourself intentional mental commands. **An intentional mental command** is a mental command that directs our consciousness, attention, and mental actions to visualize. The process of visualization may be enhanced greatly when you send intentional commands about how the process must proceed. You give mental commands about what you wish to achieve in order to receive it in reality. You need this ability in bio-energetic healing as well, which can help to increase the possibility of healing and shorten the time of healing.

Before imagining, it is always necessary to define and clarify what you are going to visualize. You can tell this instruction aloud or mentally. When you know exactly your goal in the visualization process, and give your will or thought direction, you will increase the effectiveness of your work greatly. Always help the imagination process with mentally positive statements such as "*I relax at will,*" "*Tension is leaving me,*" or "*I am in harmony with myself.*" Performing **inner mental control** over the self, you can become a master of your life. If you learn how to turn your will towards your inner-self, you will take advantage of your life, be your own authority, control your healing, and maintain **physical**, **emotional**, **energetic** and **spiritual health**.

Development of Visual Memory

Bright **visual memory** will be helpful and important in the process of imagery. Using visual memory (right hemisphere), humans reflect received information not only with words but with images, and they continue to see and work with images as they want. The ability to perceive the world with visual images is given to everybody because of the universal ability of seeing colorful and visual dreams.

However, only the very young have such memory. In school, children develop logic memory, which is directed by the left hemisphere. As time passes, the left hemisphere becomes overwhelmed with stored information, and the ability to memorize drop down sharply. As explained earlier, the human brain consists of two hemispheres: the right hemisphere - **visual** (emotions), and the left hemisphere - **logic** (mind). The brain is supposed to memorize color, smell and sound with two hemispheres. Perceiving information in this way, the brain composes **an image** in the right hemisphere and puts the image into words in the left hemisphere. Image information is memorized easily, and may be kept forever.

However, in the civilized world any information is perceived in a curtailed way. People begin keeping such information in the left hemisphere, while nothing is kept in the right hemisphere. In this way, children's visual memory may be lost.

The lack of visual memory causes feelings of missed information; the mind artificially fills in the unrecalled details to get the whole image. Visual memory demands the understanding of stored information, creativity, self-confidence, absence of stress, and a healthy psyche. Like achieving a meditative state of mind, where both hemispheres have to increase the whole brain's power, perceiving information with both hemispheres and with all senses is our goal in visual memory.

Visualization Exercises for Developing Visual Memory

1. *Empty your mind of thoughts.* Thought is energy. When your mental energy is not calmed, it is in chaos. In this condition, it is not possible to achieve a positive result in your imagery work, and you will tire easily. The total abstinence of thoughts gives you a sensational feeling of lightness and freedom.

When you visualize, use all five senses for more effective visualization. If you experience difficulty, use words of affirmation every time you visualize.

Next, find any object, and look at it in 3-5 seconds, trying to picture it on the inhalation. Close your eyes, and try to recall the visual image on the peak of breath in 3-5 seconds. On the exhalation, try to diffuse the image mentally (fading, throwing away). With practice, change the method of picturing and diffusing, velocity, and rhythm. Find new methods and mention your feelings of insight and amazement during the process of picturing.

2. *Empty your mind, and gaze on the chosen object (for example, any body part). Keep your eyes directed on the object's center and try to look at the whole thing in 3-10 minutes. Then, close your eyes for 3-4 minutes and try to recall the color image as brightly and clearly as possible. Repeat a few more times, and compare the original with the image.* Perform the exercise in a different way each time, and try to find new details. A new way of performing the exercise will lead to a condition of astonishment and lift your whole condition to a new qualitative level. Try to do this exercise with all your body parts.

3. *Gaze at an object in the same way as in the previous exercise in 3-10 minutes (or until the first thought). Turn around and look at a piece of white paper. Try to recall the image and*

place it mentally on the paper. When you have already learned how to visualize different objects or body parts, you may follow with the visual memorizing of pictures or cards.

Before every exercise, you may envision the process of visualizing that you are going to perform with the intention of a needed result. Any mental exercise without intention is less effective. Mental intention can increase the effectiveness of your intellectual and physical exercises within two-three times.

4. When you are out walking or standing in line, you may perform the following exercise. *Take a look at someone or something, close your eyes, and try to visualize the image in 2-7 seconds. When your eyes are closed, you may still move. Gradually master in the act of recalling this clear and bright "momentary photo," and keep it in your mind as long as you need.* When you have trained for a while in performing this exercise with closed eyes, you may then try visualizing with open eyes. *In this case, you look at "a photo," and see a memorized visual image with opened eyes while turning around to "see" any scene.*

5. *Choose a subject, take a look at him or her, and close your eyes. Now you hold a "momentary photo image" mentally. Try to continue the situation in mental visual images rather than stop it. Mentally pretend and follow the subject's moving or direction, then compare your result with reality after opening your eyes.* With more practice, you will be able to animate "a picture" and reduce the quantity of mistakes in comparison with the subject's real actions.

6. *Start as in exercise 4 with one exception: the "momentary photo" now needs to be moved, overlaid, and changed in its form in a determined direction. Keep manipulating the "mental photo" as many times as you need until you do it easily, without any strain.*

7. If you still need to continue the practice of keeping an "emptied mind" and brightness of imagination, you may perform the following exercise. *Choose an object or point. You may feel pleasantness or be free of emotions. Look at it without any thought (your look is concentrated on the center of the object and your vision holds the whole thing). Look as long as possible, absorbing the image into your imagination without allowing any thought to occur. When a thought comes to mind, close your eyes and try to*

visualize the image brightly and clearly. This will let you keep an "emptied mind" and increase accuracy of the image.

This exercise also helps to decrease "noise" in the head. When thoughts appear in disorder in the brain without stopping, "the noise" in the brain is on high level. Because of this "noise," an individual gets tired, forgets information, and has difficulty with visualization.

8. Now try this method of mental animation. *Imagine any animal, and let it live its own life and move in your imagery. Vivify objects in your imagination.*

This exercise is performed with closed eyes in the beginning of practice, and then, as you master - with opened eyes. *You may imagine that you are touching the object and it becomes vivified. Try visualizing actions with objects or live creatures upon your will.* It is necessary to achieve a condition of imagery when you manipulate with any imagined objects freely. While you need some time to activate imagery in the beginning of practice, you will need less and less time with more practice. Your imaginary work must be done effortlessly and creatively.

Visualization as Mental Healing

Now you have a powerful tool - your imagination, whose power far exceeds the power of will. The power of your will can also be helpful in the process of visualization.

Visualization takes place in your mind reality, not in the physical reality. Visualization works with your inner subjective reality, and through this reality it changes physical existence. When you have improved your imagination, you are able to manage your thoughts and images in a right way for you, increase your mind power greatly, and help your physical body's healing. Keeping visualization as an everyday practice, you will be able to help yourself relax the body, relieve any pain in your body, and free yourself of bad habits or addictions. You will find visualization of healing your organs a powerful aid in self-healing.

Visualization is effectively used in treating many stress-related illnesses or illnesses stemming from psychological and social factors. Visualization may develop your creativity and memory as well, and enhance your life greatly. Later in this book, you will learn how to use visualization in bio-energetic work in order to increase effectiveness and shorten time of achieving perfect results.

You may find the following exercise helpful in your future energetic work. *Raise your hands. Visualize blue energy flowing through your hands to the back of the throat chakra (clavicle level). Concentrate your attention on the blue energy color for 15-20 seconds. Send blue energy, with a clockwise spiral, from the peak of the chakra (on the back) to its foundation on the front of the throat. Visualize blue color constantly, leading it to become luminous.*

Visualization for Cleansing and Opening Chakras

You may open your chakras with the help of visualization. Advanced visualization allows your chakras to be cleansed of negative or blocked energy so they can be opened and function well. The health aura and the physical body receive energy from higher levels via chakras, which correspond to and are activated by the seven rainbow colors. This means that red activates the root chakra, orange activates the sacral chakra and so on.

Root Chakra and Sacral Chakra

Stand facing north, keeping your hands down. Take a deep inhalation on the count of three, and draw in your anus with the breath. Pause the breathing for three seconds while holding the anus tightly. On the count of three, make an exhalation through the mouth, returning the anus to its normal, relaxed position. Do not overstrain. This exercise is performed in tranquil rhythm for 2-3 minutes, warming up the two lower chakras.

Next, imagine mentally that you let go of bio-negative (bad or blocked) energy from your root and sacral chakras through your legs with clockwise spirals out of your body. Visualize the chakras in the forms of energetic cones with their peaks located on the spinal column, whereas their foundations come out on the lower abdomen. A red energetic spiral flows from the peak of the root

chakra down in a clockwise (as you see yourself from outside)
direction through the right leg and then goes through the ground.
An orange energetic clockwise spiral flows from the peak of the
sacral chakra down through the left leg. Imagine that negative,
stale or stagnant energy is leaving your chakras, as well as
everything that prevents chakra healing.

Cleansing chakras by throwing out bad energy is the most
important thing in any kind of chakra healing. In our teaching, what
we first need to do is throw away bio-negative energy. When the
chakra is cleansed, it can start functioning later by itself. If you feel
you need an extra energy boost, try the following exercise.

Mentally imagine how energy through both legs (red
through the right leg, and orange through the left leg) is rising to
its chakra accordingly. Mentally send energy to the peak of the
cone (foundation of the chakra), and then lead it from the back to
the front with a clockwise spiral through the chakra cone to its
foundation. During the exercise, visualize color constantly until the
appearance of the chakra's bright luminous color.

Solar Plexus Chakra

Stand facing north, and breathe calmly. Command
mentally: "Bad, bio-negative energy, stale energy is flowing out of
my solar plexus chakra with a clockwise (as you see your visualized
image from outside) yellow spiral through both legs. My chakra is
cleansing itself." Visualize yellow spirals flowing from the chakra
through both legs.

When the chakra is cleansed, you may add some yellow
energy by the following exercise. *Raise your hands with palms in.*
Mentally imagine yellow energy flowing from the cosmos through
your hands and spinal column to the peak of the chakra cone on
the back, and twist the energy with a clockwise cone spiral to the
cone foundation on the front (an inch up from the belly button).

Throat Chakra

Stand facing north. Visualize how blue energy flows with
two clockwise spirals from your throat chakra on both sides through

your hands out. Help the process of cleansing with the mental command, " Bio-negative, blocked blue energy is leaving my throat chakra, and the chakra is cleansing itself."

Third Eye Chakra

Stand facing north. Visualize a dark blue energy spiral spinning out of the third eye chakra in a clockwise direction through both hands. Help aid the cleansing process with mental instructions about throwing away harmful bio-negative energy. When cleansing occurs, send a mental blue ray through your raised hands to the back of the chakra (where the head and neck connect). With a clockwise dark blue cone spiral, twist energy to the front of the chakra's base. Visualize dark blue energy becoming luminous and bright.

Heart Chakra (Mental Body)

You may start this exercise when you have mastered all previous exercises. *Stand facing north. Visualize how bio-negative green energy spirals away from your heart chakra through both hands, allowing your heart chakra to cleanse itself. Help with the mental command: "All that blocks the chakra and prevents its healthy functioning is leaving. Anahata chakra becomes opened and functional."*

Send a yellow energy ray to the peak of the solar plexus chakra cone (chakra base). Next, send a dark blue ray to the peak of the third eye chakra cone. Visualize colors brightly and clearly. Command yourself mentally, "Energy from my two chakras must flow to the heart chakra without any hindrance."

Start sending visual energy from both chakra cones to their bases on the front at the same time. Follow energies from the front chakras to the heart chakra (going down from the third eye chakra, and going up from the solar plexus chakra) mentally. Visualize how two energetic colors - dark blue and yellow - meet at the heart chakra on the front and blend spirally into green, becoming bright gradually.

Central Chakra

Stand facing north. Visualize violet bio-negative energy spiraling out from the Central chakra and passing through the left leg into the ground. Your chakra becomes freed from bad energy, and then starts functioning. To add more violet energy, visualize all other healthy working chakras with their individual colors on the spinal column. Next, visualize energy spirals clockwise from the back chakras, the two upper and three lower chakras, to the heart chakra through the spinal column. All color energies meet at the back heart chakra and blend into a violet energetic knot. Send this violet energy from the peak of the energy cone to the front of Central chakra with a clockwise spiral. Try to visualize bright violet color.

Development of the Crown Chakra

Stand facing north. Visualize a white energetic spiral with all negative energetic information flowing out of the crown chakra into the cosmos.

Next, have a seat in the Lotus yoga pose, or sit simply with crossed legs. Close your eyes, and put your fingers together. Imagine that the Moon (feminine, cold energy) is located on the left side, and the Sun (masculine, warm energy) is on the right side, and there is an ocean of cosmic energy around. Start pulling in visual moon energy through the left nostril. Raise this energy to the third eye chakra, and then to the crown chakra. Next, let it down on the left side of the spinal column to the coccyx. At the same time, pull the Sun energy into the right nostril, and leading it through the third eye chakra and the crown chakra, let it down on the right side of the spinal column to the coccyx. At the coccyx, the energies unite and make three spiral coils up: moon energy rising on the left side of the column, sun energy rising on the right side. The two rays meet on the back of the head (area of hypothalamus), the energy rays cross over. The moon energetic ray goes to the right hemisphere, whereas the sun energetic ray goes to the left. The energies' rays meet at the crown chakra. Mentally, make an energetic knot.

Repeat this exercise 10-15 times, raising energies on the inhalation, and letting them down on the exhalation.

Exercises with Visualization
White Light Healing Energy

With the following exercise, try to direct the healing energy of **White Light** to your physical body. Stay disciplined, and try to practice this exercise believing in successful results.

1. Sit on a chair and relax your body, keeping your spine straight. Try to achieve full relaxation. Mentally imagine how a flow of White Light enters the crown chakra and then spreads over the whole body. Almighty White Light fills the diseased organ and dissolves toxins and ill cells into subtle substances, which speed away with White Light's flow to your feet. Then, they are thrown out of the body into the ground.

2. Visualize White Light entering the crown chakra and acquiring an auric egg form. Imagine the self inside this auric egg. The energy of White Light starts circulation in your auric egg or energy system, and your breathing becomes even and calm. Mentally, create bubbles from White Light. These subtle balls surround your chakras and penetrate them, entering your physical body. Beginning at your third eye chakra, imagine how a bubble of White Light enters and surrounds your head. Imagine similar light balls entering all other chakras from the head to the root chakra. Try to observe this process with your inner sight. Your blood flow is recharging now with vital energy, and your nervous system is stimulating.

In the process of meditation, your inner voice announces: "I am surrounded by White Absolute. Every cell of my body is like an antenna receiving energy and giving it to my whole physical body." You also may chant the mantra, "A-O-O-O-Y-M..."

Chapter Four

The Ether "Double" Image
as Energetic Information

Using the Pendulum
To Measure Chakra's Energy

Galaxies can be spiral, and the universe is composed of spinning wheels of energy. Energies pass in the form of waves in space. Kundalini rises spirally to the crown chakra. Chakras are spinning and energy spirals through chakras while they are in good condition.

We cannot see these energy movements, but we can see its manifestations. We can evaluate our chakras and measure their openness and their health. A chakra's spinning or stopping, as we will observe, can tell us about its condition. Furthermore, chakras' spinning can be measured as patterns of bio-energetic activity and the energetic flow of prana (healing, flowing energy) entering chakras.

As prana is considered **bio-positive energy**, everything that prevents the **bio-energetic balance** (any congested, stale, stagnant energy or energetically harmful information) in the energy system is **bio-negative energy**. In bio-energetic healing, bio-negative energy may be recognized in the forms of energetic signals such as tingling, electric shocks, coldness, subtle heaviness, or any other signals. Unusual signals or negative energy in this case shows imbalance in the bio-energy system. Later, when we practice with a tool for measurement chakra's energy flow - **the pendulum** - we will need this definition to recognize any imbalance in the energy system.

To assess degree of flow, its bio-positive or bio-negative direction, and to determine its quality and strength of energy, we use a pendulum. A pendulum may be made from a crystal, ring, nail, or any other thing hanging on a chain, by cord, or any thread. With the pendulum's help, we can grasp energy flows around the chakras. The pendulum is used as an assessment and diagnostic tool in energetic healing. It gives clear evidence of energy flowing through the chakra system. It moves as energy spins and spirals in the chakra. When holding a pendulum, we can feel the degree of movement, its velocity, and the smoothness or ease with which it spins or swings around. All these characteristics describe energy flow in the chakras or bio-energy systems. In this way, we may determine the quantity and quality of energy flows in the chakra by observing the direction and "shape" of pendulum movement, allowing for assessment of a human organism on the energetic level.

An advanced healer always feels any sluggishness or subtle hesitance of pendulum movement over chakras, which can tell a lot about the energy flow. Later, with more practice with the pendulum in our chakra healing method, you will also be able to feel any subtle uncertainty of the bio-energy flow showing an imbalance in the system.

When a chakra is opened and functional, a pendulum spins over the chakra in energy's natural positive spin - clockwise. Any negativity reverses the course of a pendulum from its natural flow, putting it into a negative spin. When a pendulum moves counterclockwise over a chakra, it reveals the bio-energetic negative state of the chakra's energy. Any pain or tension will indicate itself in the energy pattern someplace in the body; chakras of that area will be affected. When a pendulum is still, it shows that the chakra is closed and dysfunctional, for energy does not flow through a dysfunctional or blocked chakra. This chakra state leads to pathology in the physical body because of imbalances in energy fields and lack of energy on the physical level.

Sometimes energy flows through the chakra, but there is an imbalance in the flow or in its quality, causing the pendulum to move in an ellipse rather than in a circle. Pendulum elliptical, or any uneven movement, indicates energy imbalance in the chakra. Pendulum swinging shows that energy is blocked in the chakra because of negative thoughts and attitudes. We ourselves can close chakras off subconsciously through fear or other strong emotions, turning away from things, or holding back. When this happens, we pull the energy into the body, causing heaviness, depression, or blocked muscles. Pulling energy in causes emotional blockage of chakras, which we may observe as pendulum swinging.

Making a Pendulum

To work with chakras, you will need to make a pendulum of your choice or buy it in a special store to use for assessing your bio-energetic state. For our favorite version of the pendulum, we take an ordinary black thread and needle, and put the thread through the needle (Figure 4). We make seven knots on the thread, symbolizing seven chakras. Through the end of the needle, we put a toothpick, securing it on the needle. (You will easily feel and even see any subtle hesitance or sluggishness of the energy flow while observing the toothpick moving.) On the end of the thread, we fasten another toothpick so the hand can hold the tool comfortably.

The advantages of our pendulum are lightness, sensibility and simplicity, important qualities for effective work on the energetic level. Such a pendulum is very susceptible to bio-energy, even to the most subtle energetic signals. Anyone can work with this pendulum, even if he or she does not possess a strong and developed bio-energy field.

To work effectively with chakras, you have to get used to your pendulum. You have to like it and feel pleasure working with it, never tension or negative emotions. *While working with the pendulum over the chakras, there is a union that occurs between your physical, mental, and intuitive subtle bodies. You may try to put the pendulum over your chakras and see the pendulum movements as your chakras spin or move.* This is a common way in chakra healing; most energy healers do this. *You may hold the pendulum over your palm (a minor chakra). You will observe its clockwise movement if the chakra is functional. When you put the pendulum on the other side (over your hand), you can see the*

Figure 4. Pendulum

pendulum in a counterclockwise movement, because chakras move counterclockwise on the back.

Later, we will show you how to assess and heal chakras by our own method, which has never been known or used before.

Practice with the Pendulum

Before any bio-energetic work with your pendulum, you have to learn how to operate and command over your pendulum. This kind of exercise is needed to get more practice, gain confidence in working with the pendulum, and to feel the power of your mental body and mental energy. In contrast, you will need to learn how to work with your pendulum without any intentional mental commands, and how not to influence the pendulum at all in order to observe and measure the energy flow in reality.

*If you want to ask questions regarding a person that you do not see at the present time, you may take white paper and place your pendulum over the paper. Visualize this person as brightly as you can (as a full photo of the whole person), and place this image on the paper before your eyes. To receive correct answers, you have to keep the whole person's visual image in your mind during the procedure, reduced to the paper size. This is a phenomenon of mental energy. You ask questions and receive answers in yes-and-no fashion from the person's energetic informative field. If an answer is "**yes,**" the pendulum will spin **clockwise** (positive); if the answer is "**no,**" the pendulum spins **counterclockwise**.*

The person you are talking with is somewhere far away right now; nevertheless, his or her subtle energetic bodies are answering your questions. This phenomenon is as opening doors to other bio-energetic phenomena, which are connected not only with human's bodies and bio-fields, but with their energetic "**phantoms,**" or **ether "double" images**, as well.

*Now bring your mind into a meditative state; you need to practice more with spinning the pendulum. Work with your **mental energy** (the energy of your mental body) rather than with chakras at this time to check energy movement.* As we know, human consciousness can control and command over human energy. We can increase mental energy flow, and we also can change its direction mentally. Thought is energetic in its nature. Let's observe this.

Hold your pendulum over a piece of white paper. Do not *move your pendulum intentionally. Next, say aloud, "Spin clockwise." With these words, you have to give the pendulum a strong mental command to spin clockwise. Do not strain your brain.* If your mental body is developed, the pendulum will spin. Your energy has to be accumulated on the fingertips when holding the pendulum. Your mental body will help the pendulum to start spinning. You must be sure the pendulum will start moving clockwise upon your mental command. It begins to move in response of your mental thought as a result of the response to the electromagnetic energy flowing through you. *To compare, you may then let the pendulum move intentionally by your physical action. Feel the difference between intentionally spinning and spinning with your mental help.* You do not really need to help it intentionally, because the pendulum "listens" to your strong mental will without any physical action.

After you became comfortable with the clockwise spinning of your pendulum, you may try counterclockwise spinning (help with mental and voice command as well). Next, swinging the pendulum with your mental command helping with voice command is a good exercise also. When you have learned to move the pendulum mentally in different directions, you may start to practice stopping the pendulum motion at once with the command, "Stop." All these exercises have to be done without any physical help or movement of the hand or fingers, on the mental and energetic level.

Next, try to perform all these exercises without any voice command, by mental intent only. Mastery in performing of these exercises will prepare you to work effectively with your pendulum on the energetic level in order to assess your energetic or physical states or even these of others.

If you can do nothing in the beginning, do not give up. *Try to develop your mental and intuitive subtle bodies, the throat chakra, and the third eye chakra.* With more practice, you will be able to manipulate the pendulum. We are energy beings. The ability to manipulate by bio-energy is given to us-you just have to open and develop it.

When you have mastered the pendulum's moving and stopping, you are ready to perceive the chakras' energetic signals.

All these exercises with pendulum mental control prepare you to become a master chakra healer who "turns off" his or her extrasensory abilities, all mental commands, any influence on the pendulum, or even any subtle physical action when he or she does chakra assessment by pendulum. The task of a master healer is not to influence the pendulum by her or his highly developed energetic subtle bodies, but to be an independent expert in the chakra system assessment. By learning to avoid influencing the pendulum by your mental, intuitive, and other subtle bodies' energies (which can interfere with the process of chakra assessment), you can perceive the correct energetic information about your physical and emotional conditions or these of other people. Otherwise, you may affect your pendulum work with your bio-field without even realizing it.

To practice the non-influence of your pendulum, you may perform the following exercise. *Relax your physical body* (by this time you should have already mastered in the relaxation of your physical body at will and by meditation), *calm your mind and bring it into the meditative state as specified in Chapter Three without any interfering thoughts. Visualize the person you wish to "look" at energetically, reduce the image to the paper size, and place the image on a white paper. Hold the pendulum over the visualized image. Never strain your brain (you must feel lightness and ease in the head to perform such work). Do not think about the pendulum and its movement. You must not give any command to the pendulum; only gaze on the paper with the image and notice any movement of the pendulum: clockwise spinning, counterclockwise spinning, swinging, or a still state.*

Be sure that you do not influence the pendulum. If your pendulum does not move in the beginning as it is supposed to do, it indicates the presence of your energetic and mental blocks. It is important to be in a trance-like brain condition (thoughtless, independent, or meditative). Try to practice this exercise often and with different images to achieve mastery, an unusual brain-state of a total "turning off," and the ability to work comfortably with the pendulum.

Drawing the Ether "Double" Image

As stated earlier, an individual's **ether "double"** contains his or her complete energetic information including all organs, parts, and systems of the physical body. Whether healers perceive energy in a healee's bio-energy field at a close distance or any long distance, they "deal" with the ether "double" body. Performing bio-energy healing, healers work with the ether "double" of the physical body, at first perceiving its energetic information and imbalances, and then cleansing, balancing, normalizing, and healing the energy fields. Healing and normalizing imbalances on the ether level brings health, vital energy and balance to the physical body.

When performing a distant energy healing or assessment, healers keep the visualized healee's energetic image before their eyes. In this way, the healer controls over the healee's energy field and conducts healing with his or her mental energies. Then the healer can construct the visualized healee's energetic image on a paper in order to perform bio-energy assessment and healing.

The next step in our method of the chakra healing is drawing **an ether matrix - the ether "double" image**. *When you take a piece of white paper and hold the pendulum over the paper, the pendulum does not move because the paper does not signal energetically or even contain any energetic information. Nevertheless, when we "place" an energetic image (energetic matrix) of a visualized person on this paper, the pendulum starts moving, perceiving the bio-energy of the ether "double" image.*

The pendulum is very sensitive to bio-energetic fields. When we visualize a live person and "put" the image on a white paper, the pendulum will spin clockwise. In a case of visualizing a dead person, the pendulum spins counterclockwise, indicating a lack of live or balanced energy.

While continuing to visualize, draw an individual's image you wish to assess energetically on a white paper using a pencil (Figure 5). *When you draw an image, do not try to draw it professionally; this is not the point. Give a will to your mental and intuitive subtle bodies to do this, and follow you intuition in the process of creative drawing. Your drawing is energetic in its nature because it reflects an energetic image of the visualized person.*

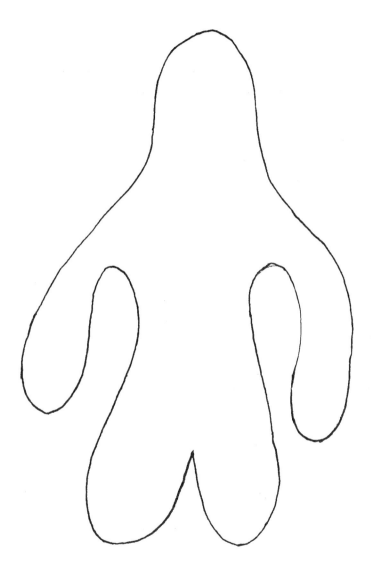

Figure 5. Ether "Double" Image

Here is the technique for drawing the ether "double" image, the energetic matrix of the person's ether body whose energy state you are going to assess. *Relax, visualize the person, and start to draw his or her image with a pencil.* Drawings of people will be different every time because of the variety in personalities and energetic states. With more practice, you will see that difference in the thickness or length of drawn hands or legs indicates different states in the physical bodies (for example, whether the condition of extremities is disturbed). The position or uneven form of a drawn head may describe energy irregularity and imbalance in the area. Or, irregular or uneven lines of the drawing may indicate a stressful condition in the energy field. With practice, you will find that all details of drawings are important for describing some aspect of energy information. Your individuality gives you a personal style in drawing as well. As an energy healer can perceive his or her own energetic signals and symbols while assessing the bio-energy field, with intensive practicing you may perceive forms of an energetic image in your personal energetic interpretation.

After you become comfortable with drawing, you may pay attention to the smoothness or irregularity of your drawn contours. In time, your intuition will allow you to interpret more symbols into energetic messages. *Observe the contour and pay attention to the signals that come through your inner process of the mind.* With the intensive practice of drawing energetic images, you will master in energetic communication.

Energetic communication, like verbal communication, consists of transmitting and receiving information. **Codes**, **symbols**, and **patterns** of information are involved in energetic communication as well. Sometimes difficulty occurs in energetic communication because of differences in **decoding**. Meaning of the energetic symbols and codes is the conscious connection between them and patterns in your consciousness. This is why determination of your consciousness' patterns in coding and decoding energetic symbols is important. Symbols may remain stable, but their meaning may be changeable in your intuitive body as you progress. Energetic communication is a creative process. We offer our own way of energetic communication and decoding, whereas you may find your own meaning after much practice. *Be sure to take notes of your* *observations while working with the pendulum over your energetic image and observe patterns of your thoughts and insights.* It is an exciting way of exploration.

For example, *draw an image of your own ether body, visualizing your own reduced image at the moment of drawing yourself. What you have on the paper now is your ether "double" image. This image is energetic in its nature and reflects your energetic state at this moment. When you draw someone else, you "place" his or her visualized and reduced image. The image reflects an energetic state of the person, which you have drawn, at the present moment.* It is a phenomenon in bio-energy teaching and healing. On the drawn image of the ether "double" body, you can measure the energy, and determine the energetic and physical state.

When you have finished drawing the image, you may check the energy with your pendulum. If your pendulum spins clockwise over the drawn and visualized image, it shows a good energetic shape and physical health in general. If you observe counterclockwise movement, you may decode that an energetic imbalance or negative energy is present in the bio-energy field, and physical illnesses are present on the physical level. This general exercise prepares you for the more complicated energetic work coming later in this book.

The General Chakra Assessment

The next step in drawing the ether "double" image is placing the energetic centers, or chakras, onto it (Figure 6). *Onto your completed drawing, sketch the chakras as small circles on the person's image.* The pendulum will help you to assess the chakras on the energetic image, revealing energetic disturbances and showing energetic symbols that you need to decode to glean information about the chakras' states.

Start the chakra assessment by working with your pendulum over each chakra on the ether "double" image, beginning from the root chakra and finishing with the third eye chakra (the crown chakra is not assessed on everyday basis, but is always drawn in its place).

Place the pendulum over the chakra. If the pendulum starts

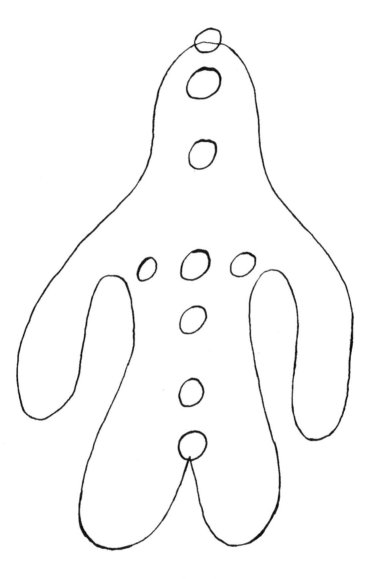

Figure 6. Placing Chakras onto Ether
"Double" Image

spinning clockwise, it means the chakra is opened and working in good condition. *In this case, pay attention to the diameter of the spinning and the movement's smoothness,* which can tell you a lot about energy strength and its quality in the chakra. When the diameter is greater, than energy level is greater.

When the pendulum is spinning in a counterclockwise direction, the chakra is dysfunctional or closed, indicating the presence of stale energy, negative energy or energy imbalance. This negative energy leads to inflammatory processes on the chakras' physical level. On the emotional level, it brings about negative characteristics in a person's individuality (described in Chapter Two) and emotional problems. The swinging of the pendulum in any direction indicates energy blocks or emotional blocks. Elliptical or uneven movement shows energetic imbalance in the chakra. And if the pendulum is not moving at all, the chakra is closed and totally dysfunctional. A closed chakra is the result of prolonged stress or accumulation of negative energy in the chakra. In turn, the chakra causes stress, a low energetic level, physical illnesses and any other disturbances in the physical body.

Wholeness of the Ether "Double" Image

Your advanced mastery in visualizing and your deep understanding of energetic processes now permit you to have an energetic contact and communication with energy fields and chakras through the ether "double" image. What you will do now is entirely possible and real when you have prepared mentally and intuitively for energetic work. When you understand this practice and can use it in everyday life, you will see a life with a new set of eyes. You will intensely understand its energetic magnificence, and its ability to work for you in all areas of being. When you have mastered in visualization of an image, placing the image mentally on paper, and drawing the person's ether "double" image with chakras, you can do the following procedure.

On the top of your drawing, write the person's last name, first name, and date of birth (including date, month, and year) (Figure 7). *By writing this information, you usher the energetic*

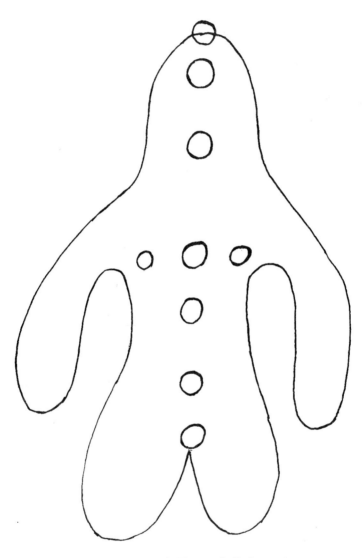

Figure 7. Person's Energetic Information

information of the person into the image drawn on the paper.
The image before your eyes now belongs exactly to this person. This person's image with written energetic information reflects his or her energetic and physical condition at the present time. This is one of the miracles in energy healing that we have discovered and practiced for years. There are many people on the earth with the same names or birth dates; nevertheless, you have exactly the same person whose energetic information you wrote and whom you want to assess on the paper now. Now you have completed your ether "double" image to work with on chakra assessment and healing.

On such an energetic image, you may easily assess the chakras' performance, the energetic and physical condition of yourself, your family members, or even pets. Moreover, you will be able to perform chakra healing. Whenever you feel low, tired, stressed, painful, depressed, or "unbalanced," you need chakra and energy assessment and balancing. You can help yourself with your drawn ether "double" image and your pendulum to recognize all imbalances and disturbances in your energy system and on the physical level, and heal yourself by opening your chakras, removing energetic blocks, and balancing your energy.

Bio-Energy Defense

Before working with bio-energy fields, it is important to learn how to perform **bio-energetic self-defense** and to use it every time you work with bio-energy. Self-defense must to be done to avoid any energetic interfering of bio-systems at energetic contacts, especially their bio-negative influence on each other. There is an opinion among energy healers that in order to avoid being enervated in energy healing after a close encounter, one must stay emotionally uninvolved in the bio-energetic process. However, this is not enough. Bio-energy fields interrelate even without intentional cooperation. Someone's negative attitude or constant thoughts may depress your energy system and enervate it if this person is constantly close to you. When you are involved in the bio-energetic processes of healing, besides the possibility of becoming enervated, there is a possibility to acquire the same energetic and even physical problems as your healee.

Because of this threat, you need to perform bio-energetic defense. We have described the methods of bio-energy defense in our book *Health by Bio-energy and Mind*, and how to use them in everyday life. Being energetically protected means that you are protected from any intervention of someone's bio-negative energetic information or energy. Thus, energetic defense allows you to avoid negative emotional and stressful interfering with others energy systems.

Dealing with an ether "double" image may be the most safe method of energetic assessment and healing, because much of your work is done with energetic information on the **"energy informative" level**. Nevertheless, make it a rule of thumb to perform bio-energetic defense when you work energetically to avoid problems with energy fields interfering.

Here is a method of self-defense called **the Yoga Lock** (Figure 8) for working carefully on the energetic level. *Put the fingertips of one hand on the fingertips of another, but in the reverse order (one thumb is put on the little finger, another thumb is put on another little finger, and other fingertips are put accordingly). One palm faces your chest, and the other palm faces away from the body. While keeping the lock, tell yourself mentally: "My illnesses do not transfer to you, and your illnesses do not transfer to me."* After performing this technique of defense, you can practice your energetic work without encumbrance, interference or depletion of energy.

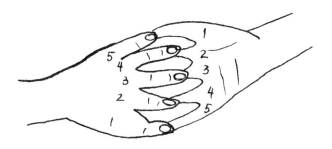

Figure 8. Yoga Lock for Energetic Defense

Chapter Five

Ether "Double" Image Chakra Assessment

General Chakra Assessment
on the Ether "Double" Image

Chakra assessment shows the energetic, emotional and physical conditions very precisely. During the assessment of a person's image chakra system, you will perceive the energetic, physical and emotional conditions of this person. You can determine the condition of the chakra system as a whole: if an individual's chakras work perfectly and spin in their natural way (clockwise), he or she is in good energetic, physical and emotional shape. When chakras are closed, dysfunctional, blocked, or unbalanced, they need healing.

Healthy people have opened and functional chakras; you can check this on the completed ether "double" energetic image. Nevertheless, even healthy people may have temporarily blocked chakras or imbalances. *To assess chakras in this way, as stated earlier, write the last name, first name, middle name, and month, date, and year of birth of the person you want to assess (it can be you as well).* Now you have the energetic identical information about the person on the paper. *Next, draw a person's energetic "double" image with chakras*; these chakra images reflect the "real" ether body's chakras. Now get out your pendulum to assess the person's energetic and physical condition, weak organs, energetic imbalances, and even illnesses.

At first, start the **general chakra assessment** *by the placing the pendulum over the root chakra (the first chakra) and following with the next five chakras. Observe the movements of the pendulum over each chakra. Take notes about the chakras' states, listing observable symbols of pendulum movement for each chakra and your sensations for further detailed assessment.* This completes the **general assessment on the front side of the chakras**. If the pendulum showed clockwise movement over all chakras, indicating that all chakras are opened and functional, there is no reason perform **the chakra assessment on the back**. (When a chakra is in working condition on the front, it is functional on the back as well.)

To assess the chakras from the back, draw the person's picture again and write the full name and birthdate as usual. Write "the back" on the top of your drawing to give command for perceiving energetic information from the back.

Repeat the chakras' assessment on the back beginning with the root chakra. The natural spinning of chakras from the back is in a counterclockwise movement (Figure 9). If chakras are spinning in any other way, they are not working properly or they are closed and need cleansing. *When holding the pendulum, always check the diameter, degree of the pendulum movement, velocity, smoothness, and the ease with which it spins around.*

If you observe that the chakra is dysfunctional either on the front or the back, it means you need to perform **a detailed assessment of the organs or body parts** that correlate with the chakra on the physical level. With **a detailed chakra assessment**, you may determine what organs or body parts have an energy imbalance or are weakened physically. When we discover any energetic imbalance in the system, it indicates physical discomfort or illness on the physical level. Each chakra influences organs, body parts, and systems located in its area. When the chakra is healthy and working properly, it influences organs, body parts, and systems of its area in a positive way, bringing health and vitality. However, closed and dysfunctional chakras also affect the health of their correlated organs, parts, and systems, bringing in imbalances and illnesses.

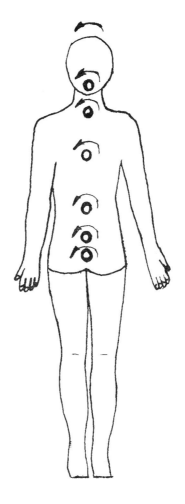

Figure 9. Chakras' Natural Movement
From the Back

Here is a list of the chakras and their corresponding organs, body parts, and systems.

Chakras and their Physical Correlations

Root chakra: penis, groin, testes, vagina, anus, bladder, coccyx (tailbone), bones, and the sexual and reproductive systems.

Sacral chakra: spleen, ovaries, adrenal glands, uterus, kidney, urinary tract, lower abdomen, large intestines, appendix, sacrum, sexual system, and energy level.

Solar Plexus chakra: musculature, pancreas, stomach, liver, gallbladder, small intestines, blood sugar, lower, middle, and upper spine, diaphragm, upper abdomen, solar plexus, and digestive system.

Heart chakra: lungs, windpipe, breast, chest, ribcage, bronchi, heart, circulatory and lymph systems, blood pressure, esophagus, shoulders and shoulder blades, mucous membranes, immune system, and thymus.

Throat chakra: throat, vocal cords, ears, nose, mouth, jaw, neck, shoulder clavicles, sciatic nerve, legs, feet, knees, arms, elbows, hands, thyroid and parathyroid, skin, respiratory system, colds, and sinus allergies.

Third Eye chakra: eyes, sinuses, headache, forehead, autonomous nervous system, pituitary gland, cerebrum (the part of the brain responsible for senses, visualization, and verbal/auditory), cerebellum (the part of the brain responsible for motor coordination, reality contact, balance, dizziness, and the epilepsy center), brain stem, and the hypothalamus (the part of brain responsible for stress response).

Crown chakra: central nervous system, pineal gland, hair, head top, cerebral cortex (the part of the brain responsible for thinking), and mind agility.

On the back chakras, it is better to assess **the whole spinal column** (the spinal column corresponds to several different chakras). You may assess all other organs on the back chakras in the same way as on the front.

For example, say you are checking someone's root chakra.

If it is working on the front, it is working normally on the back also. The physical condition of the lower abdomen is healthy, and all organs correlating in this area to the first chakra function perfectly.

When you have discovered which chakras are dysfunctional or unbalanced, you need to perform a detailed assessment of organs or body parts in the areas of these chakras.

Detailed Assessment of the Physical Organs

For the detailed assessment, you draw the ether "double" image with specific organs or body parts belonging to the area of the dysfunctional chakra. For example, for a dysfunctional sacral chakra you draw the organs which correspond with this chakra (you may draw as many drawings as you need, separating or combining some organs on the image drawing to assess them comfortably and properly). Draw a chakra on each organ to insure that you receive the exact energetic information you need from this organ. Pass your pendulum slowly over each drawn organ. When you perceive a positive energetic signal (clockwise spinning on the front) from a specific organ, you know that this organ is functioning well. If a perceived signal is negative (counterclockwise movement on the front), it means this organ has an energetic imbalance or disturbance that can cause weakness or illness. If the pendulum is still, it means that the organ is already weakened and possibly unhealthy, and needs healing.

When you have mastered visualization, you may draw organs under only the written energetic identification mentioning the name of the organ while corresponding organs mentally to the person's ether "double"(Figure 10). To do this, *write the person's energetic information and the organ's name on the top of the drawing, and draw the chakra on the organ or body part.* By doing so, you connect the energetic field of this ether "double" with the organ's energetic field. Thus, you may perceive and interpret energetic information from this energetic part or organ and assess the energetic state, determining which organs retain an energetic imbalance and perceiving possible energetic information about negative energy of weak organs or body parts.

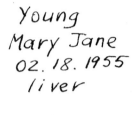

Figure 10. The Organ's Ether "Double"
Image with One Chakra

Figure 11. The Organ's Ether "Double"
Image with Three Chakras

When you assess an energetic condition on a drawing with many physical organs, put one chakra on each organ or body part. However, to achieve a more precise assessment, you must put at least three chakras on the organ or body part (Figure 11). By doing this detailed assessment with three chakras on the organ, you may determine even which part of this organ is unbalanced or disturbed on the energetic level.

You may also *draw one part of an organ for a more detailed assessment (put chakras and energetic identification on it as well). Pass your pendulum over the organ, body part, or its cut, and remember or list energetic symbols and signals for prospective healing.*

To make a quick assessment, draw pictures of the body parts and organs you are interested in before your assessment, and then, when it is needed, write the energetic identification of the person above the drawings. However, do not try to make copies of images. Your images must be "live" with your energy to talk to you on the energetic level, at least in the beginning of practice. With serious and intensive practice, you will be able to inspire an energetic life into copies as well.

Dysfunctional Chakras
and Body Malfunctions

Dysfunctional, closed, and blocked chakras can lead to and cause physical illnesses. People with terminal illnesses always have depleted root chakra. People with a low energy level have a dysfunctional sacral chakra. People with regular headaches have an unbalanced or dysfunctional third eye chakra. People with digestive problems have a dysfunctional solar plexus chakra. People with throat problems who get regular colds have a dysfunctional throat chakra.

Besides an organ assessment, you can distinguish some illnesses on the physical level. Let us classify some illnesses and their correlation to dysfunctional chakras. (However, our book is not intended as a prescription or diagnosis, or as a replacement for professional medical help. Seek a doctor's help for illnesses or any acute problems.)

Such malfunctions as obesity, hemorrhoids, constipation, physical weakness, arthritis, prostate enlargement, bladder problems, reproductive problems, and menstrual cramps are correlated with **dysfunctional root chakra**.

Kidney illnesses, spleen problems, impotence, frigidity, uterine bladder problems, food cravings, toxins in large intestines, and gas pain are correlated with **dysfunctional sacral chakra**.

Ulcers, diabetes, hypoglycemia, digestive problems, liver problems, hiccups, and burps are correlated with **dysfunctional solar plexus chakra**.

Asthma, high blood pressure, breathing allergies, cough, lung's illnesses, heart problems, and immune system illnesses are correlated with **dysfunctional heart chakra**.

Problems with arms, hands, legs, feet, mouth, thyroid, flu, neck ache, headache, allergies, skin problems, sore throat and sinuses, ears problems, and nausea are correlated with **dysfunctional throat chakra**.

Blindness, eyes' problems, headache, migraine, colds, brain-physical and brain-psychological problems, addiction and obsession, brain stem problems, and nightmares are correlated with **dysfunctional third eye chakra**.

Depression, distress, alienation, confusion, mind agility, and hair problems are correlated with **dysfunctional crown chakra**.

Distress and Chakras

We mentioned that the third eye chakra and the crown chakra are responsible for psychological problems, stress reaction, distress, and depression. However, we have observed during our long years of experience that distress and depression in turn cause all other chakras' dysfunctions.

We cannot imagine our lives without stress. We encounter many stressful situations every day: traffic on the road, personal relationships, job interviews, not having enough time, communication with others, sleep disturbances, and various other extreme situations. As people and their attitudes differ from each other, their reactions to stress are wide and varied.

Our inherited ability to react to threat or danger with a series of biochemical changes in our organisms on the physical level (**the fight or flight response**) helps us deal with extreme situations. These biochemical changes, made by the sympathetic nervous system, increase heart rate, breathing rate, metabolism, muscle tension, and blood pressure, as well as decrease blood flow from the extremities (legs and arms), and digestion. Prepared in this way, an organism becomes ready to fight or run from an external event. When the stressful situation has passed, the organism returns to its normal state.

Relaxation response occurs as the organism returns to its normal state, releasing stress, strong emotions, and tension. The relaxation response mechanism turns off the stress response in this way: the brain stops sending signals to the organism about the hazard, and in minutes metabolism, heart rate, breathing rate, muscle tension, and blood pressure return to normal levels. If the mind and body cannot reach relaxation response and the stress response condition continues uncontrolled, it can cause secretion of corticoids by the adrenal glands, which inhibit digestion, reproduction, growth, tissue repair, and so on.

When stress becomes **distress** ("negative" stress) and lasts for a long time, all chakras close and become dysfunctional or blocked. If this stressful condition is prolonged and the mind still receives signals of threat, the mind will continue to keep the physical body aroused. This causes energetic **bio-negativity**, energy flow imbalances, and the presence of stale or stagnant energy. All other subtle bodies contract, because they can no longer communicate and receive vital energy through closed chakras. Moreover, the chakras cannot function at all when people stay in prolonged stress (distress) because their chakras become congested with stale or stagnant energy, or overcharged through unexpressed strong emotions and even expressed strong emotions.

When the chakras are closed, dysfunction can occur at the physical level. A distressful physical body state affects one's whole energetic system, and in turn, the whole energetic system, when dysfunctional and low energetic-wise, influences the physical body. On the physical level, chronic stress and a disturbed energetic state can increase the occurrence of many illnesses and weakness in the physical body. Chronic stress and energetic imbalance can cause muscle tension, fatigue, hypertension, migraines, ulcers, or chronic diarrhea.

Closed, blocked, or dysfunctional chakras and conditions of the whole human bio-system lay marks on the person's destiny, character, communication with others, and well-being. Many people live with closed or dysfunctional chakras due to consistent stress. In such energetic conditions, they may experience anxiety, fear, depression, weakness, unhappiness, dissatisfaction, insecurity, emotion suppression, indifference, inability to express feelings, and inability to love and trust. With closed and dysfunctional chakras, people cannot communicate with others effectively, or have success in any commencement or career as well.

Why do people have continued distress? Distress causes the chakras to close, and then closed chakras prolong distress in turn. In a case of distress, chakras cannot open and cleanse themselves naturally. We must cleanse and open our chakras by ourselves, help any bio-negative energy, tension and strong emotions to be released, stabilize bio-energy, and restore psychic, emotional and physical health.

Emotional and Mental
Issues and Blocks

As we have stated, our emotions, thoughts (our subtle bodies) and physical well-being are closely linked and interrelated. First we must change our attitudes about ourselves and our lives. Energy follows our thoughts. When we feel good and positive about ourselves, we cause good and positive things to happen in our bio-energetic systems, our subtle energetic bodies, and then in our lives. When we become more positive and affirmative, our energy changes in a positive way, and we feel good and energetic. An effective way to decrease the possibility of distress in our lives is by integrating positive activities and optimistic moods and thoughts into everyday life.

In order to weather negative stress and to have lower frequencies of illness or weakness, people have to view difficult situations and threats of life from a positive point of view - as challenges, possibilities to prove or examine themselves, or opportunities for personal growth. People who can cope with negative stress undertake stressful events and stressors in a positive way while getting life experience. They can neutralize distress and make positive conclusions from negative experiences. Moreover, these people can stabilize their energetic health while recovering from distress. On the physical level, coping with stress begins from an awareness of one's own body, analyzing any states of tensions, aches, and physical sensations. On the energetic level, coping with stress or any irregularity begins with discharging blocked, stale, stagnant, and negative energy from the bio-energy system.

The roots of human problems spring from the energy conditions of their bio-fields. Negative thoughts, strong emotions, and inappropriate physical actions are energy problems. However, energy problems can occur because of the energetic influence of others as well. Bio-energy systems interfere with those of others and influence each other. In this way, others' bio-energy systems can bring problems to one's own system. "**Bad eye**" or "**energy damage**" can be introduced into one's energy system by others as well. Brought intentionally or accidentally, such an "energy damage" or "bad eye" conveys negative energetic information into one's bio-system, piercing subtle bodies and forcing chakras to close. This can happen during communication with upset or angry people because of the intersection and interference of subtle bodies during a highly charged conversation.

Our negative thoughts and emotions bring negative bio-energetic states of energy, even if we have not received it from the outside world. Our own negative thoughts and attitudes can block vital energy flowing in our subtle bodies and physical bodies. People with low self-esteem and self-confidence tend to pull energy into their systems, particularly negative energy, since low self-worth is negative. People with low or negative self-characteristics hold back energy in their chakras, creating **energy blocks**. They do not release negative energy, but accumulate it in the energy systems. These energy blocks prevent people from having positive relationships and from fulfilling and enjoying their lives. With blocked chakras, people do not have full access to their vital energy, leading to negative states of mind, confusion, and depression.

How do energy blocks occur? When children are told they are bad, dull, uninteresting or by other negative terms, they create mental, emotional, and even physical blocks for themselves which, later in their lives, causes fears, inactivity, doubtfulness about their abilities, loneliness, and numerous pains. Any blocks show an alteration in destiny that prevents one from fulfilling one's life purpose. While blocks can be provoked by a physical problem, negative emotion, wrong mental belief, or unexpressed feeling, it can affect the whole human system.

Physical blocks reflect any disharmony or disturbances in the physical body such as diseases, pains, or any physical problems. Physical blocks often prevent us from physical activity, causing mental and emotional blocks and deteriorating our feelings. These negative feelings and beliefs can, in turn, deteriorate our well-being.

Mental blocks are beliefs that prevent us from developing our inner selves toward peace and spirituality. Mental belief is a powerful "mechanism" which can affect our well-being, attitudes, emotions, and actions through either positive and negative thoughts. Mental and physical healing can be manifested through positive, affirmative thoughts, whereas, negative thoughts bring energetic imbalances, blocks, and illnesses. The mental body, as the strongest body, has forceful impact on the physical body. We are what we think. The implications of negative or false beliefs programmed into mental patterns bring continued damage until the physical system is fully destructed.

Often people suppress strong feelings and emotions, storing them inside themselves. Such repressed feelings or emotions become destructive for energetic, physical, and psychological states. It is not healthy to hide feelings and emotions inside us, but we often do this, afraid to express any feelings or emotions if they seem different from accepted norms. Suppressing or hiding of any feelings or emotions or their absence at all can cause **emotional blocks** and prevent creative development or growth as well.

Spiritual blocks stem from a misunderstanding about our inner-selves, our spiritual connections with the universe, and our place as cosmic organisms in the universe. Spiritual blocks are the most complicated blocks. A misunderstanding of our life purpose on the spiritual level leads to disconnection of our spiritual (cosmic) selves from the Divine Source. When spiritually blocked, spiritual selves lose the power of uniting their bodies, minds, and souls into cosmic organisms. They are not able to maintain the health of our cosmic organisms or to carry their special mission upon this plane. Spiritual blocks about our own "true essence" lie within our souls. The soul records the emotional, mental, and communicational experiences and events in all our lives, and it imprints beliefs about these experiences, aspects of life and death, selves and others, and good and bad in our temporary physical bodies as well.

The main cause of many of our blocks or chronic unsatisfactory states and behaviors is the result of unhappy experiences imprinted on our subtle bodies in moments when we were highly receptive or suggestible, particularly in childhood. These blocks may remain stable in us for a long time, for our whole lives, or even extend into future lives unless released or cleansed.

We need to choose positive thoughts, positive and confident feelings about ourselves, and meaningful relationships with our inner-selves and with others to avoid presence of constantly blocked energy in our bodies. Our brain states and behaviors are not beyond our control. We are not powerless, and we are not victims of our beliefs, our past, our feelings or our environment. We can change states intentionally, quickly, and at will. We can choose the healthiest way of handling feelings - releasing them or letting them go.

We can only benefit by discharging blocked or negative energy from our bodies through healing and cleansing our chakras on a regular basis. Healthy chakras not only give us the possibility of increased self-awareness, emotional stability, mental clarity, and spiritual growth and maturity, but also the ability to heal ourselves and others. In the next chapters, we will show how you can always be freed of negative or blocked energy in a new and innovative way so you can maintain your health and the health of your loved ones.

Chapter Six

Ether "Double" Image Chakra Healing

Advantages of Ether "Double" Image Chakra Healing

We offer a unique opportunity to heal people effectively without their direct participation in the process of healing, and at any distance. Distance in our method has no meaning; there is no distance for energy. Our method of **Ether "Double" Image Chakra Healing** is possible because the energetic matrix possesses an energetic connection with an individual to be healed. This matrix reflects his or her energetic information and physical state at the time of the assessment and healing. This is how our method of energetic healing differs from others — it allows the healer to work with an individual at any distance and in an expansive aspect of the human energy field that is not possible with other methods.

With our method's help, it is possible to positively influence and maintain people's physical conditions and health on a regular basis, and even prevent any physical illness or heal already existed imbalances without touching or giving any medicine. We can easily work in all the areas of bio-energy system to bring balance. With our method of Ether "Double" Image Chakra Healing, we can work on all chakras, major and minor, on the physical body or out-of-body, and on all subtle bodies as well. We can work on any physical organs, body parts, and body systems. We can relieve negative stress, negative thinking, and depression or any emotional discomfort. We can relieve any mental disturbance or condition, bringing peace of mind and optimal mental health.

Our method of chakra healing is also safer than many other healing methods. A chakra healer in direct contact with a healee has to be physically, emotionally and energetically healthy, and his or her aura must be thoroughly cleansed of energetic negative information and in balance. However, many healers can heal themselves very rarely, if at all. Healers themselves may be enervated, stressed, or have high blood pressure or any number of imbalances in their own energetic systems or physical bodies, which they may pass with their energy to the healee. Whereas in the method of Ether "Double" Image Chakra Healing, everyone has a possibility to heal the self and maintain his or her energetic and physical health before helping others.

Withdrawal of Bio-negative Energy from Chakras

When we discover closed, dysfunctional or blocked chakras, our primary task is to cleanse them of everything that prevents healthy functioning and let the chakras function normally. *In bio-energy and chakra healing, the most important thing is removal of weak, ill, congested, or blocked energy from chakras and subtle bodies rather than bringing in new energy.*

When people are less spiritually developed, they tend to bring more energy in than they give out. During illness, they may acquire energy from more energetic or spiritually developed people. These people are called energetic sappers. They accumulate vital energy with their negative energy, and still have imbalances and blocks. Vital energy, when added to negative, stale, and stagnant energy, loses its value. Prana is only really vital for humans when it enters clean, functional chakras and subtle bodies developed in their growth. Healing by energy and chakra healing bring energetic health when vital energy is brought into an already cleansed and balanced bio-system.

People who are not very developed in their spiritual growth may also be open to negative forces. Negative energy or negative information comes into their chakras, causing them to feel even worse than they do or to act in even more negative ways. Negative forces cause energy damage, imbalance, and dysfunction on the energetic level, whereas on the physical level, bio-negativity causes chronic illnesses and permanent weakness. On the emotional level, people become unstable emotionally, unexpressive, secluded, unfortunate, or aggressive and malicious.

On the other hand, evolved and spiritually developed people have more energy flowing out of their energy fields than flowing in. They cleanse and balance their energy, and then radiate it out. People with high energy have immensely colored auras or even overbalanced (whitish) auras. When people feel peaceful and joyful, their energy flows out, radiating from their bodies and opening their chakras. As long as the energy flows or spirals away from the body, people exist at a refined emotional and energetic level. If the energy spirals back into the body, it can cause a negative or stressful reaction. When chakras are cleansed, opened and functional, they bring as much energy to the bio-energy system as it needs and filter the energy appropriately for the bodies' use.

Any pain or tension will indicate that something is going wrong with the energy flow somewhere in the body. These areas of energetic "tension" or congestion will affect chakras, causing them to close, and will show an imbalance in the energetic state.

Energy in blocked areas tends to release. If negative, stale, or stagnant energy is not released, we may feel depressed and have low energy. In our stressful times, we need to perform chakra cleansing periodically. When we go with it, work with it on an everyday basis, and allow it to continue the energetic cleansing, it will not be long until we are feeling very good again.

For chakra cleansing, we offer our **method of energetic spirals**. With the spirals' help, we draw out any bio-negative energy away from the chakras, cleanse them, and normalize the chakras' healthy energetic regime. To do this, *draw spirals in a clockwise movement **on the front of the ether "double" image drawing**. In the beginning of practice, along with drawing spirals, use mental affirmations and visualizations during energetic healing work.*

Through the simple act of drawing spirals, real chakra cleansing will occur.

On the same front drawing of the ether "double" image, draw spirals in the following way. Start drawing a spiral from the dysfunctional chakra by moving your pencil clockwise and going down the leg, if it is one of the three lower chakras (Figure 12), *and going down the arm if the chakra belongs to the three upper chakras* (Figure 13). *Coming out the chakra, the spiral ends with an arrow and comes into a drawn square. A square symbolizes means a door to the cosmos where we can throw bio-negative energy away, possibly to be cleansed or balanced on a higher cosmic universal level. Energy comes into the squares with the clockwise spiral movement of your pencil.*

To cleanse the crown chakra, draw three clockwise spirals starting from the chakra, whirling up, and finishing with arrows (Figure 14). This procedure will help to access the White Absolute and energetic cosmic information through the chakra. *To cleanse the ground chakra, draw clockwise spiral from the chakra whirling down, and finishing with arrow* (Figure 14).

After drawing spiral withdrawals, check the chakras again with the pendulum. Depending on the degree and quantity of bio-negative energy in the chakras, you will observe the clockwise pendulum movement immediately, or in the not-too-distant future.

When you assess chakras with the pendulum after drawing the energetic spirals, and you observe that the particular chakra starts working but still feebly, hold the pendulum over the chakra and spin the pendulum in clockwise circle movements, intentionally coiling up energy in the chakra to help the energy flow. This will help the chakra work once it starts to be cleansed of bio-negative energy. You may use this technique after throwing away bad energy from all chakras with spirals.

You should not wait until you and your family do not feel well - *do chakra cleansing for yourself and your family regularly* in order to keep an energetic balance, keep your chakras opened and functioning perfectly, and to fill organisms with vital energy. When chakras are opened and functional, they let in vital energy and regulate the energy flow for optimal energetic, physical, mental and emotional health and balance.

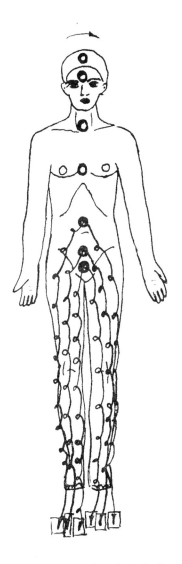

Figure 12. Drawing Spirals from
Lower Chakras

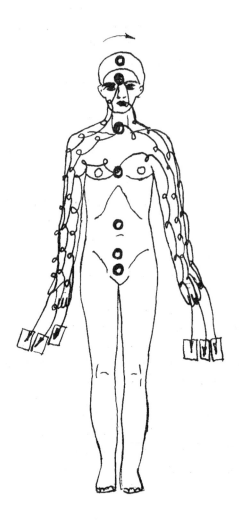

Figure 13. Drawing Spirals from
Upper Chakras

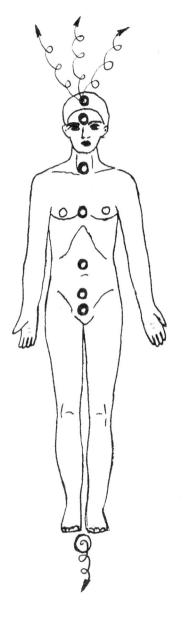

Figure 14. Drawing Spirals from Crown
and Ground Chakras

*After cleansing the chakras on the front of the ether "double" image, we need to cleanse them **from the back** as well* (Figure 15). *Because you are working on the back, draw counterclockwise spirals, entering the squares in the same way as on the front. With every turn of a spiral you withdraw bio-negative, blocked energy and help the chakras to "turn on" and work perfectly. Lead the spirals through the arms from the three upper chakras, and through the legs from the three lower chakras. From the crown chakra, draw spirals of bad energy in a counterclockwise movement through three directions as on the front. In the beginning of your energy healing practice, you may still visualize the process of throwing bad energy away and command mental affirmations to help quicken the process of cleansing.*

Remember, chakras are interrelated. *If the root chakra is not functioning well, cleanse it with the third eye chakra together (and vice versa). The sacral chakra can be cleansed with the throat chakra, and the solar plexus chakra with the heart chakra.*

Thereafter, this drawn image is cleansed from bio-negative and weak energy on the front and on the back of the ether "double" image. **Cleansing**, **balancing**, **normalizing**, and **healing** are the four stages of withdrawing weak and bio-negative energy from the chakra and bio-energy system, and all these stages come in the order as described above. When the chakra cleansing, balancing, normalizing, and healing are done on the image by drawing energetic spirals, actually energy healing work is performed on the real person. The person's real chakras are cleansed and become functional on the front and the back. The person's ether body is balanced now, and this person feels physically, emotionally, and spiritually much better than he or she did before.

We use spiral energetic cleansing, balancing, normalizing, and healing not only for chakra and ether body healing, but also for removal of any bio-negative energy from the physical organs, body parts, bruises, aches in the hands, legs, or any pain in any area of the physical body. *After you perform the detailed chakra assessment and determine which organs have an energetic imbalance, draw a circle around the weak area or pain center symbolizing the chakra, and from its center start to draw a spiral in a clockwise direction. If a suffering organ or pain center is located in the area of the*

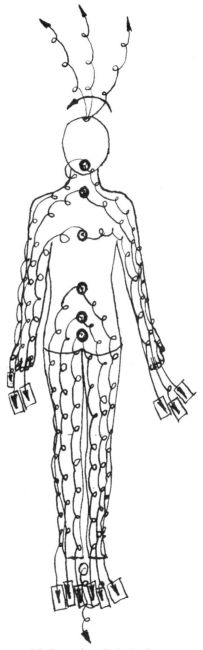

Figure 15. Drawing Spirals from
Chakras on the Back

*three lower chakras, spiral energy moving a pencil through the
ether "double" image's legs; if it is located in the area of the three
upper chakras, lead the spirals through the arms. Finish the spirals
with an arrow, and around this arrow draw a square as a symbol
of throwing energy into cosmic space.*

You have now mastered in chakra assessment, cleansing
dysfunctional chakras from bio-negative energy, and "turning on"
the chakras for their perfect spinning. If, after cleansing the chakras
with spirals, the chakras have not turned on at once, we use the
method of ushering positive energetic information into chakras.
We will describe this process next.

Ushering the Information into Chakras

After withdrawing sick energy from the chakras, *we are
going to usher positive energetic information into the chakra system
with the spirals' help.* In this way, we project a balanced energetic
state, and put into the person's ether body information of health,
longevity, and positive mood. For this purpose, *write the healee's
name and birthdate on a white paper, draw the ether "double"
image, and put the chakras on it. Positive energetic information
may be ushered with your mental affirmative help through the third
eye chakra of the person's drawn ethereal image.*

To increase the effectiveness of ushering energetic
information, we perform the following procedure. First, *draw a
square (symbolizing the cosmic doors for Prana to enter) on the
image's feet level. Rise the spiral moving your pencil clockwise,
entering the third eye chakra. While drawing the spiral, mentally
suggest health, cleansing, and longevity to the drawn person and
write these words over the spiral. This energetic information will
be ushered into the third eye chakra on the drawn image and on
the energetic level of the real person as well. Through the third eye
chakra, we receive divine energetic information* (Figure 16).

At the time of ushering the energetic information, we should
withdraw any negative energetic information still present in the bio-
energy system, for this can prevent the fulfillment of the ushered
positive information on the energetic level. *To withdraw any leftover
bio-negative information from the system, start drawing the spiral*

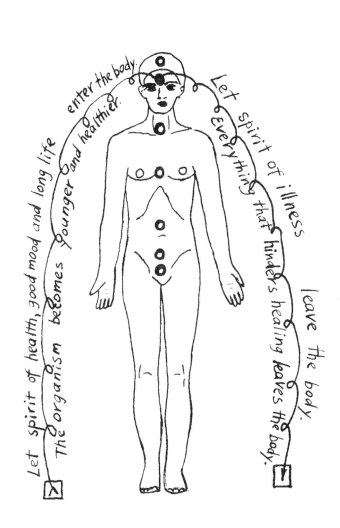

Figure 16. Ushering Information into Chakras

clockwise from the third eye chakra down, ending with an arrow concluded into a square. Write these words over the spiral: *"Everything that hinders healing must come out of the organism"* (Figure 16).

When you have mastered these techniques, you will be able to help perform self-healing and the healing of others so quickly and effectively that you will be amazed.

Energetic Chakra System Defense

This **system of energetic defense** will prolong the refined state of the chakras and defend the cleansed system from entering any negative information as long as possible. *Write the energetic identification on the top of a white paper, and draw the energetic image with chakras. Draw chakras with colored pencils, using colors in order of where the chakras belong.* Thus, **red** is used for the root chakra, **orange** - the sacral chakra, **yellow** - the solar plexus chakra, **green** - the heart chakra, **blue** - the throat chakra, **dark blue** - the third eye chakra, and **white** goes for the crown chakra.

After this, draw seven colored circles symbolizing a rainbow around the ether silhouette. Draw the red circle, follow with the orange circle that is above the red, and draw all other circles in colors accordingly (yellow, green, blue, dark blue, and white). Now you have the energetic chakra defense to deflect negativity from yourself or others. Keep this drawing as long as you need. You should renew this drawing once a month for any accumulation of bio-negative information; this will prevent the possibility of it entering the chakra system again. You may throw the drawing away, or burn it and replace it with a new one.

We recommend performing the chakra assessment for yourself and your relatives on an everyday basis, or at least on a weekly basis to find out what chakras have become closed or dysfunctional due to stress, any influencing factors, or others' energetic information. When you feel indifference in your good "form" or appearance, a low energetic state, apathy, or become tired easily, you should assess your chakras. If you discover that your chakras may be dysfunctional, fix them first with spirals to remove negative information, then usher healing information if you need it.

You may perform all these procedures for yourself, your children, family members, or even your pets. Soon you will see you can start living a new, fulfilling life, and have perfect relationships and communication. You will be able to prevent illnesses, normalize them if you have them already, and always control and maintain your **physical**, **psychic**, **emotional** and **energetic health**.

Specific Uses of the Ether "Double" Image Chakra Healing

Pains and Bruises

To relieve any pain or bruise, you need to draw spirals as shown on Figure 17 to lead negative signals out of chakras and places of pain. If the pendulum describes any movements other than circular, clockwise movements, the energetic signal is negative.

After many years of energetic work, we have discerned many specific uses of the Ether "Double" Image Healing. *For example, an ache in the knees may occur due to imbalance in the kidneys. In this case, we need to energetically check the kidneys and knees. Place a chakra on the kidney of the ether "double" image, and assess the energetic state with the pendulum. If you perceive any negative signal from the kidney (uneven or counterclockwise pendulum movement), draw a spiral through the leg, leading it into the square. After this, assess the troubled knee. When it shows any negative signal, draw a chakra on the knee and lead out weak energy from it as usual.*

If there is pain in the elbow, assess the elbow and the throat chakra as well. Assessing the elbows in the place of pain, you will perceive a negative signal. *Perform the throwing out of negative energy from the elbow and the throat chakra.*

To heal bruises on the hands or legs, it is enough to *find the place of pain with the pendulum assessment, describe this spot on the image with a conditional chakra, and use the technique of withdrawal negative energy from the drawn chakra.*

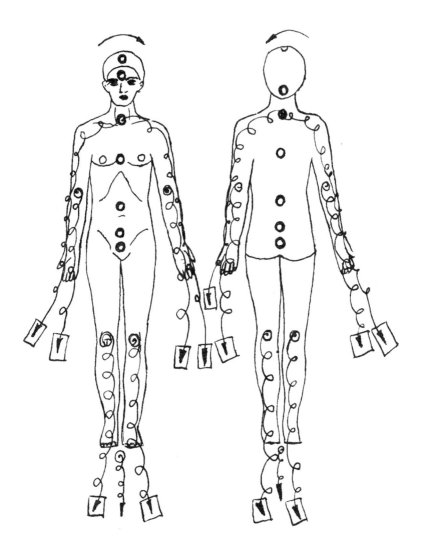

Figure 17. Pains and Bruises Relief

High Blood Pressure

To determine high blood pressure, assess the spinal column. Any tension and heaviness in the pendulum movement over the spinal column on the ether "double" image will indicate high blood pressure. *To lower high blood pressure, prepare an ether "double" image with the person's energetic information on it, mentioning "on the back." Draw a spiral leading the column of high blood pressure down, beginning from the third eye chakra through all chakras to the root chakra. On the front, perform the withdrawal of negative energy from all chakras* (Figure 18).

Low Blood Pressure

To relieve low blood pressure, it is necessary to draw a rising energetic spiral on the back of the ether image drawing, starting from the root chakra up to the third eye chakra. On the front image, perform the withdrawal of energy from all chakras (Figure 19).

Eye Tension

Assess the energetic state of the eyes by putting conditional chakras in the location of the eyes on the ether image. An eye which is disturbed will show energetic tension. *Draw spirals from the eyes' chakras relieving tension on the front of image. On the back, withdraw negative energy from all chakras with counterclockwise spirals* (Figure 20).

Carpal Tunnel Syndrome
or Overworked Hands

Withdraw weak energy (Figure 21) *from the throat chakra with spirals. Describe the hands with conditional chakras and draw the spirals from the hands' chakras as well.*

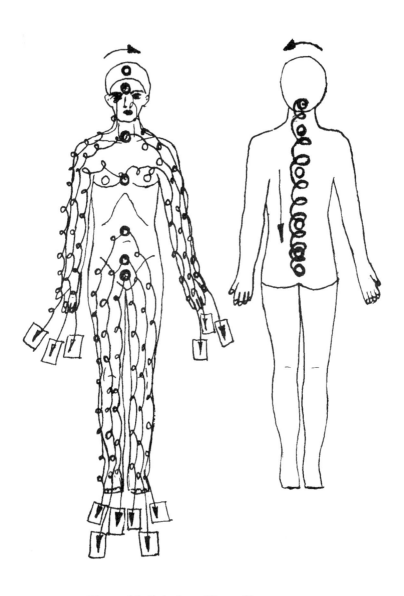

Figure 18. Spirals to Normalize
High Blood Pressure

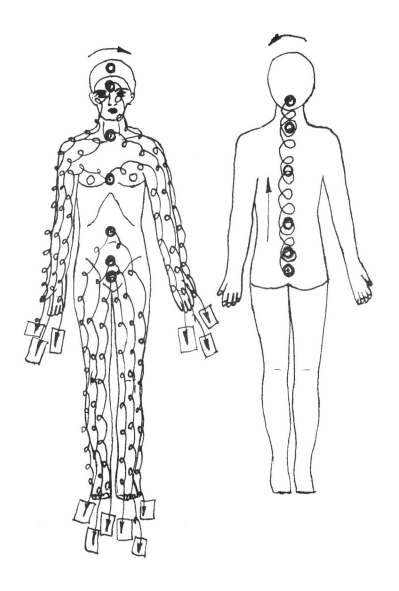

Figure 19. Spirals to Normalize
Low Blood Pressure

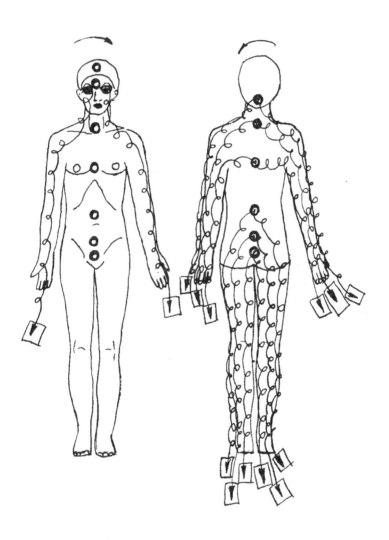

Figure 20. Eye Tension Relief

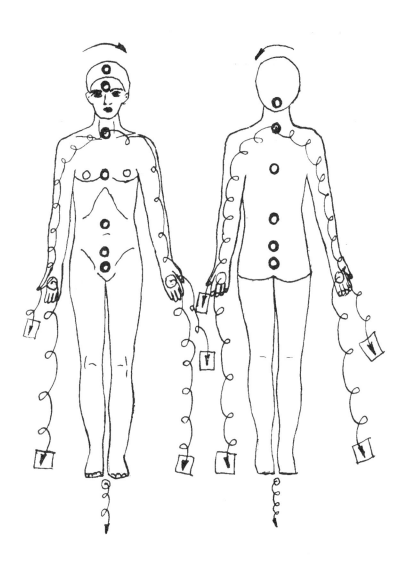

Figure 21. Overworked Hands Problems
Relief

Ear Problems (Colds)

Withdraw congested energy from drawn ears on the image as shown on Figure 22, *and from the throat chakra.*

Legs

You can "cleanse" legs in a case of painful condition and energetic disturbance along with the throat chakra (Figure 23). *Lead the spirals through the whole legs on both the front and back ether image drawings.*

Breast Feeding Problems

Check each breast with the pendulum. Draw the corresponding (conditional) chakras for the breasts, then draw the spiral from the weakened breast out as usual. Together with the breasts, we need to cleanse the root chakra, the sacral chakra, and the heart chakra with clockwise spirals on the front. On the back, lead the spirals out from the same chakras but in a counterclockwise direction (Figure 24).

Lower Back Pain

To relieve lower back pain, it is necessary to cleanse the lower three chakras with spirals on both the front and back ether images (Figure 25).

Shoulders (Nerve Inflammation, Calcium Deposits)

Cleanse bio-negative energy out from the conditional chakras described on the shoulders of the ether "double" image (Figure 26).

Heartburn

Withdraw bio-negative energy from the solar plexus and heart chakra on both the front and back ether images (Figure 27).

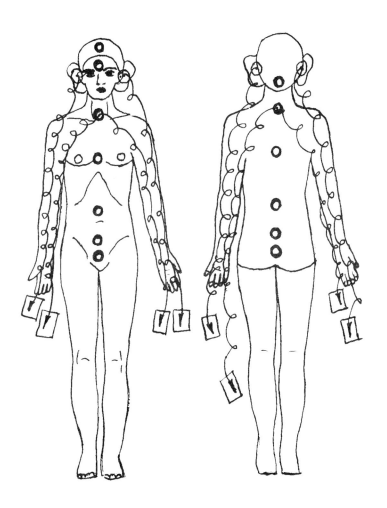

Figure 22. Ear Problems Relief

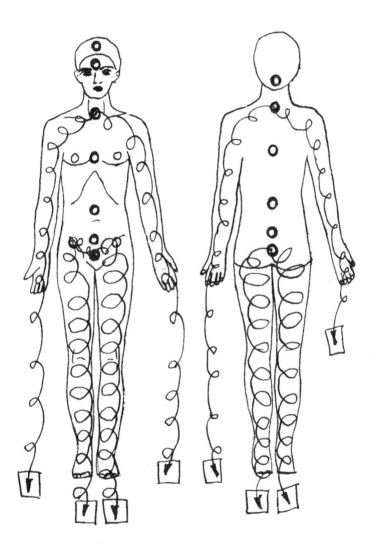

Figure 23. Legs' Dyscomfort Relief

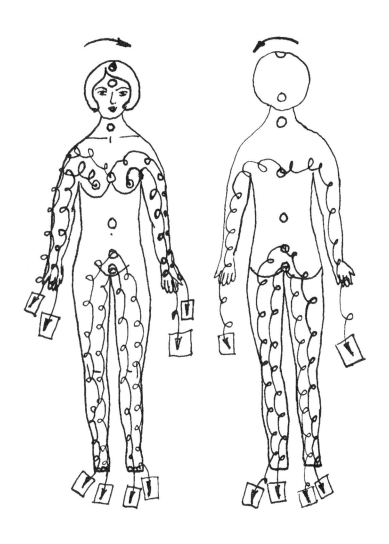

Figure 24. Breast Feeding Problems Relief

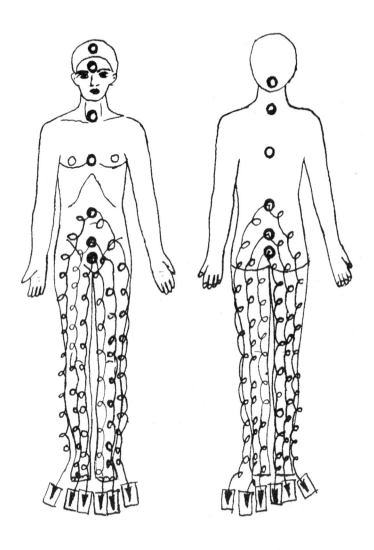

Figure 25. Lower Back Pain Relief

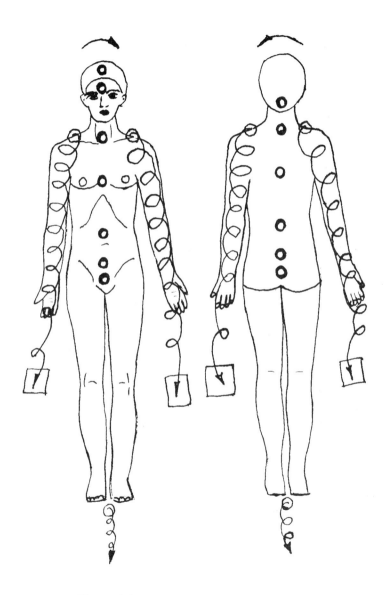

Figure 26. Shoulders' Dyscomfort Relief

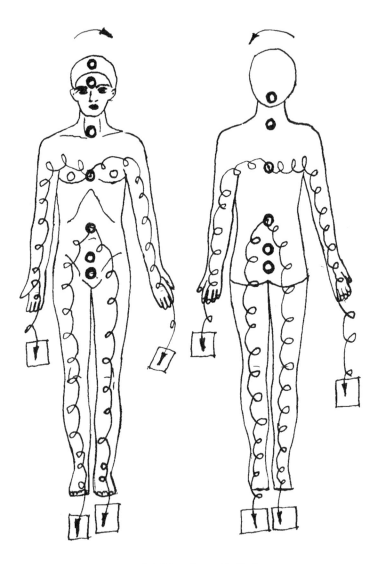

Figure 27. Heartburn Relief

Headache

To relieve headache, withdraw negative energy from the third eye chakra and root chakra on the front and back images (Figure 28), or from all chakras at once if needed.

Teeth or Mouth

Describe the mouth with a conditional chakra, and withdraw energy out from the mouth chakra and the throat chakra. On the back, "cleanse" the third eye chakra.

Toothache

To relieve toothache, draw the corresponding chakra in the area of pain. Draw spirals leading bio-negative energy from the chakra through both hands out the ether "double" image. End spirals with arrows entering squares as shown on Figure 29. Cleanse the throat chakra and root chakra as well. Repeat the procedure for the back ether "double" image.

Nose, Sinuses

Draw the corresponding chakra for the nose. Perform the throwing of negative energy away from the nose, the throat chakra, and the root chakra for the "on the front" image and from the third eye chakra, throat and root chakra for the "on the back" image (Figure 30).

Throat

"Cleanse" the sacral chakra and the throat chakra at once from both sides of chakras on the ether images (Figure 31).

Flu, Common Cold and Weakness

Withdraw bio-negative or weak energy with spirals from all chakras and both sides of the ether images (front and back as shown on Figure 32).

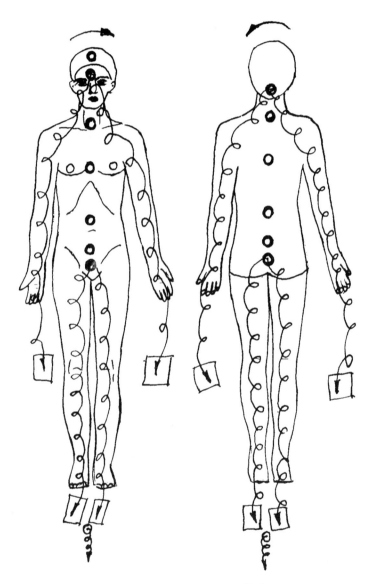

Figure 28. Headache Relief

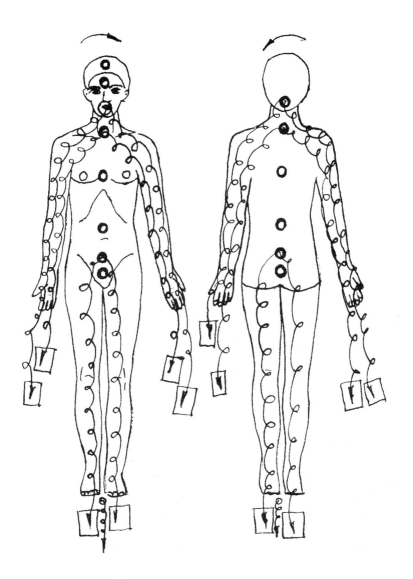

Figure 29. Toothache Relief

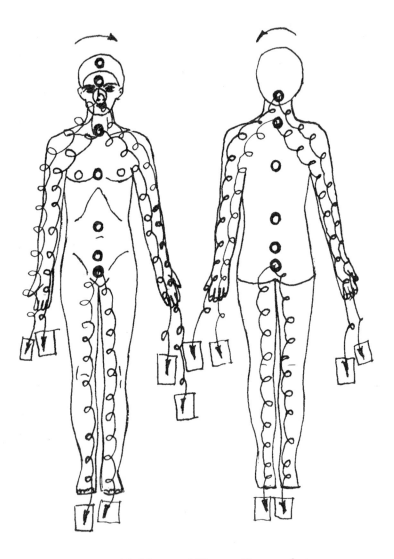

Figure 30. Nose and Sinuses Dyscomfort
Relief

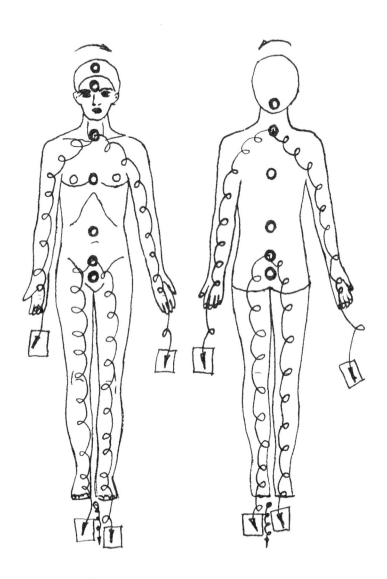

Figure 31. Throat Problems Relief

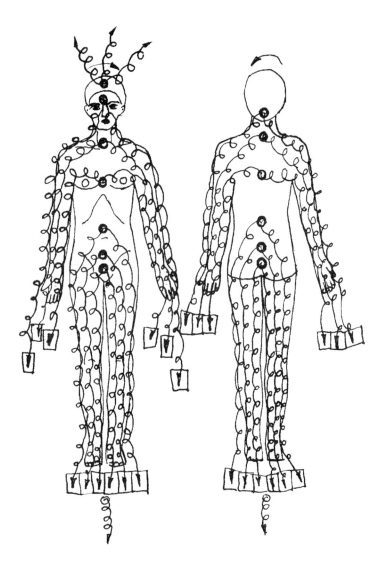

Figure 32. Flu, Colds and Weakness Relief

Withdrawal of Bio-Negative
Energy or Information

In order to maintain energetic, psychic, emotional, and physical health you must perform the cleansing of all chakras on both the front and back ether "double" images periodically and forever (as shown on Figure 32).

Liver or Intestines

When we observe energetic imbalance while assessing organs (liver, intestines), we place a chakra on the liver or intestines, and lead bio-negative energy out of the conditional chakra with the spirals coiling down through the legs (Figure 33).

Draw the spirals through the arms if the organ is actually located in the chakra's area above the solar plexus chakra, or through the legs if the organ is located in the chakra's area lower than the solar plexus chakra.

Kidneys, Bladder

In a case of energetic imbalance in the kidneys and/or bladder, place the chakras on the kidneys and the bladder. Withdraw bio-negative energy with spirals from the kidneys through the legs, and from the bladder through the legs, finishing spirals with squares as usual (Figure 34).

Lungs

Spiral energy from the drawn lung's chakras, leading it through the arms and out the ether "double" image (Figure 35).

Nervous Illnesses, Insomnia

Cleanse all chakras with spirals for the front and back ether "double" images. Usher healing information to the third eye chakra on the separately drawn ether "double" images, whereas from the other side withdraw any left negative energy or information from the third eye chakra that prevents healing.

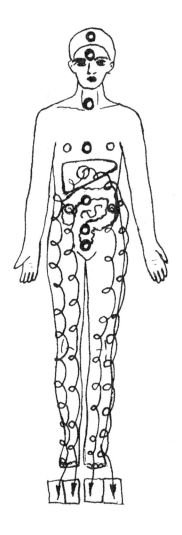

Figure 33. Liver and Intestines
Imbalances Relief

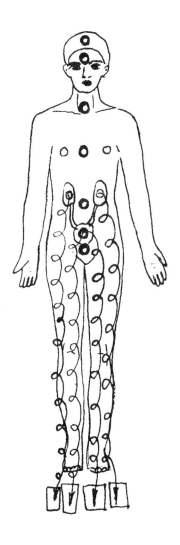

Figure 34. Kidneys and Bladder
Imbalances Relief

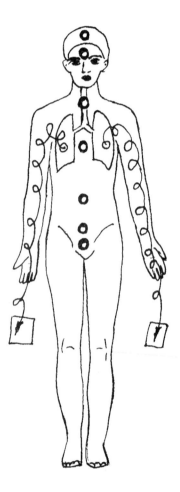

Figure 35. Lungs Problems Relief

Ushering and Withdrawal
Information in Healing

In addition to healing chakras by removing bio-negative, stale, stagnant or blocked energy, you may usher in healing information with written words into the third eye chakra to revitalize the process of cleansing chakras and confirm and project energetic and physical healing in the person's body. From the third eye chakra, lead spirals out with words of withdrawing all negative information that may stay in the system and prevent healing.

Spinal column

The condition of the spinal column is very important for the whole energetic system and general physical health. All chakras and subtle bodies link to the spinal column. All chakras divide the spinal column into areas that belong to each chakra: the coccyx vertebral region covers the root chakra and the ground chakra; the sacral vertebral region covers the sacral chakra; the lumbar vertebral region covers the solar plexus chakra; the thoracic vertebral region covers the heart chakra and the throat chakra; and cervical vertebral region covers the third eye chakra. Each vertebra reflects the same chakric characteristics as its particular chakra.

The interconnection between all chakras and the cosmos depends on the possibility of energy flowing freely through the spinal column. Spirit and matter are connected and interrelated with the help of the spine. The vertebral column supports and unites the physical body and the whole energetic system as well; so perfect spinal condition promotes both energetic and physical healing.

On the physical level, there are nerves passing through each vertebra, connecting all organs. Each vertebra is responsible for a particular organ's health. When a nerve is compressed by a vertebra, the correlated organ is affected as well. Through the vertebras, organs are "connected" to the correlated chakras and each other. On the emotional level, the condition of each vertebra affects an emotional state, and in turn emotional state can affect vertebras.

Working on a healee's spine with bio-energy of the hands, advanced healers can determine which organs have energetic and physical imbalances by way of perceived energetic signals. Every vertebra signals in a negative way if there is an imbalance in the particular organ correlated to this vertebra. Healers can place an "activated" energetic finger of one hand on the organ, and use a finger from the other hand to find the correlating vertebra, searching for an energetic signal of correlation between the correct vertebra and the organ. Then, both the organ and this vertebra can be healed.

In the case of ether "double" image healing, nevertheless, we assess the vertebral column independently, concentrating on each vertebral area or specific chakra vertebral region in addition to chakra assessment to find out even subtle imbalances in the ether and physical bodies.

Draw the ethereal image of the spinal column along with the person's energetic information. With the pendulum, assess each vertebra, or at least the chakric area or each vertebral region on the spinal column of the ether image, to find the vertebras or vertebral regions which signal with negativity. If the healee complains about a specific area of the spinal column, you will find an energetic imbalance in that area (lower, middle, or upper spine). *"Cleanse" the chakras on the "back" image as usual* (Figure 36). *Work with all lower chakras on the image to withdraw weak energy, or all middle chakras or all upper chakras when pain exists in a particular area of the spine.* Moreover, as with lower chakric dimensions, often spiritual dimensions are involved. If there is imbalance in the lower chakra, chakric area, or vertebral area, you need to check and heal its upper counterpart (chakra, chakric area, or vertebral area) on the top of the spinal column as well in order to achieve the balance in the energetic system.

In addition to chakra "cleansing," if you find imbalance on any vertebra or vertebral region imbalance on the "back" ether image, draw a chakra in that place and withdraw blocked energy from this troubled area by moving the spirals counterclockwise on the back. This procedure will be especially helpful in freeing physical and emotional blocks which easily pull us out of energetic equilibrium, or have already affected the spine on the physical level.

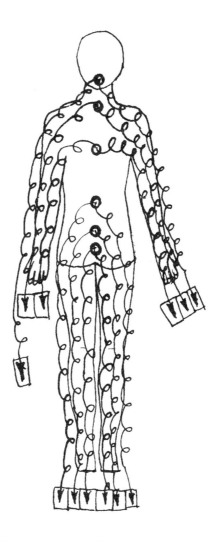

Figure 36. Spinal Column Imbalances
Relief

Chapter Seven

Ether "Double" Image Color Chakra Healing

Colors and Aura

When performing chakra healing, it is important to aid the healing with colors. **Colors** are waves of different lengths (measurement in space) or vibrations and frequency (measurement in time or speed). Any planet in the Universe radiates its own color as any living organism's **aura** or chakra does. People who are clairvoyant may perceive these beautiful "colored" energies and see colorful auras around others. Every person has personal nuances of aura colors because the whole aura is a result of development of all human subtle bodies. The greater our spiritual growth, the brighter and larger will be aura. Clairvoyants may see dark gray or black spots on the aura, which indicate energetic imbalances in the bio-energetic system and physical illnesses. When one dies, the aura disappears.

Our universe is filled with universal energies radiating from the Divine Source, bringing **universal light**. **White prana** from the universe influences our well-being, and it refracts into the seven colors of the spectrum in our organisms, as light refracts and disperses into seven visible colors when it passes through a prism. Each color represents a particular portion of the universal light, has its own vibration, and comes to us through the crown chakra in varying frequencies by the way of the psychic centers on the bodies. These seven colors are seen radiating from our physical and subtle bodies and passing through each chakra.

Vibrational energy of all colors influences our bodies positively, supports healing and removes blocks within the energy fields and chakras. In terms of vibration, chakras are zones of highly concentrated energy which are connected to various locations and areas in the bodies. As energetic beings, we are susceptible to both positive and negative vibrational or color effects of bio-energy in our lives. Differences in vibrations affect well-being, mood, emotional condition, and the brain state.

All organisms, cells, and atoms exist as energy, and each form has its own **frequency** or **vibration**. Energy vibrations bring either a sedating or stimulating effect on the stream of energy through any organ, causing a natural biochemical reaction. The various organs of the body also possess functions of sedation, stimulation, or neutralization through their characteristic frequencies. When the different parts or organs vary from these expected normal vibrations, the physical body becomes either diseased or does not function properly. When the energetic/element balance within the body is distorted, physical diseases occur in the body. All illnesses originate on the ether plane in the forms of energetic imbalance, and these imbalances then affect body organs and systems on the physical plane.

Energy bodies can be healed by **the energy properties of colors**. As the color rays accelerate in frequency, their **wavelengths** are shortened and they influence humans in different ways. For example, the color red has the longest wavelength and the lowest vibratory rate of the visible spectrum, whereas violet has the shortest wavelength and the highest vibratory rate. Thus, red is the "densest" of all colors and is always closer to the dense physical body. Violet is the most subtle, and it is closer to the white Absolute.

You may assess the chakras' and subtle bodies' colors by evaluating the conditions of the chakras with the pendulum, noting the intensity or diameter of the pendulum's spinning. The dominance of one color over another occurs when functional chakras dominate over the dysfunctional at the time of the assessment. Such information must be given an accurate evaluation before you can conclude the chakras' influence over the personality. If the chakra itself needs stimulating or sedating, its own color can be used to draw the chakra and spirals to remove negative or blocked or stale energy. Each color used in chakra healing motivates chakra cleansing and balancing energy. However, colors should not be overused in drawings because of the possibility over-energizing.

Colors may be used more effectively in our systems when we know the qualities and characteristics of each color. There are more than seven colors that are correlated to the additional human subtle bodies and chakras, however, we will employ major colors in this book, which will be useful in our Ether "Double" Image Chakra Healing method.

Energetic Properties of Colors

Red

Red, which is the first color of spectrum, correlates to **the root chakra**. Red has the lowest vibratory rate in the color spectrum. The root chakra brings red color in our auras, producing vitality on the physical plane. Red (waves, energy), with its lowest vibratory rate, corresponds to **the physical body** and to the most solid aspects of the physical body such as bones, muscles, tissues, sinews, and blood.

Red is a physical energizer and a stimulating color. The quality of red in the root chakra indicates the degree of force, vigor, and vitality in the organism. An overactive root chakra or too much red in the root chakra shows aggressiveness, spite, and irreconcilableness. A normal working root chakra (bright clear red) shows generosity and personal warmth.

Orange

Next in the color spectrum is **orange**. Orange is a warm, vitalizing, and nourishing color. It is an energizer, healer, and equalizer. As the energy of **the sacral chakra** and **ether body** (our energetic home), orange is a stimulating color for our energy systems' strength. Orange is a more tender color than red because of its higher vibratory rate. The sacral chakra has more movement and is more complex than the root chakra due to its orange frequencies.

An overactive or dark orange sacral chakra gives activity, provocative behavior, pride, and selfishness. A clear orange or normal chakra provides vitality, health, self-control, balance, and consideration of others.

Yellow

Yellow is the third color in the spectrum. Sunny yellow, with its vibratory rate, relates to **the solar plexus chakra** and **the astral body**, which control our emotions. Whereas thoughts and emotions are conceived in the mind, they are felt in the solar plexus ("brain" of the nervous system). Yellow gives stimulation for the nervous system, regulates emotions bringing the ability to feel joy and laughter, and also activates the mental faculties like memory, ability to study, analyze, and be a positive thinker. Yellow represents intellect, wisdom, knowing, and self-esteem on the personality level.

A normally working solar plexus chakra, bright yellow in its color pattern, gives optimism, intelligence, business skills, spirituality, happiness, and lack of worry. An overactive or dark yellow chakra shows indecision, personal weakness, jealousy, suspicion, and impracticality.

Green

Green is nature's master color, which represents a balance of all colors as well as chakras. Green, as a blend of the yellow (wisdom) on one side and blue (truth) on the other, is the color of peace, harmony of nature, renewal, refreshment, and nurturing love. It is the color of growth. Green resonates with the heart area, **heart chakra**, and **the mental body**. It acts as a neutral link between lower vibratory rate energies (warm colors), which represent more active or physical levels, and higher vibratory rate energies (cold colors), which represent spiritual levels. Green gives peace and calmness to the mind and is a great tonic for the spirit.

A normally working, bright green heart chakra represents independence, peace, regeneration, freedom, success, prosperity, healing, thoughtfulness, versatility, and adaptation. An overactive, dark green chakra shows fear, envy, and religious fanaticism.

Blue

Blue is a higher frequency color than green, being the more spiritual one. If lower vibratory rate energies are stimulating energies, blue, as a high vibratory rate color, is the first in the spectrum with a sedating effect. Blue balances earthy energies and spiritual energies. By its frequency, blue relates to the **throat chakra** and **karmic body**. Blue represents spiritual awareness and inner peace. Truth, devotion, and dedication are qualities of blue. Blue is an electromagnetic cooling color; it brings coolness, control, and detachment, and vibration of lightness as well.

A normally working, blue throat chakra provides self-reliance, accomplishment in work, inspiration, confidence, loyalty, sincerity, and devotion. An overactive, dark blue throat chakra shows hardiness in attempt to achieve a goal, depth and dedication, or egotism.

Dark Blue (Indigo)

The next cooling color in the spectrum is **dark blue** or **indigo**, one of very high spiritual vibration. Indigo relates to **the third eye chakra** and the forehead area on the physical level. It is also the color of the **intuitive body**. If blue is a healing color that balances earthy energies, indigo is the universal healing color. It lends spirit harmony, tranquillity, and clarity. Indigo awakens inner knowing, helping to find answers intuitively from the inner-self rather than from analytical reasoning. Indigo leads us to the necessity of growing gradually into a consciousness level where the higher frequency can be more easily assimilated. It brings relaxation and meditative state of mind.

A normally functioning, indigo third eye chakra gives intuition, integrity, spirituality, a deep level of the inner-self, sincerity, and devotion. An overactive, dark indigo third eye chakra indicates an ability to heal, clairvoyance, and a search for deeper meanings in life.

Violet

The highest frequency color before White Absolute (the blend of all colors) is **violet**. This color of **Nirvana body** (Universal Love) is the color of kings who belong to their people with all their hearts and souls. It is the most spiritual and meditative color belonging to the individual, indicating that this individual is already united with the universe. Violet is correlated with the soul.

White Absolute

White Absolute is the white light of **the crown chakra** and **Absolute body**. It is the color of the light coming from the universe. White Absolute, as a circuit of creation and love, is the most subtle substance in the universe. The flow of white universal light enters the crown chakra and then spreads over other chakras, bringing wisdom and spiritual vibrations. The blend of all rainbow colors creates the summary white. White represents perfection of development and spirit receptivity. Spiritually developed people may have whitish aura or predominant white color of their bio-fields.

Chakra Assessment Using Colors

As the colors of an aura tell us about the personality in its present state, so do the characteristics and "amount" of chakra colors in the energetic image. A pendulum spinning impulsively in a diameter larger than an inch over the root chakra on a person's energetic image means overabundance of red in chakra energy. This may indicate a despotic nature, aggressiveness, nervousness, and difficulty in relaxation or concentration. An overactive root chakra (dark red) also brings spite. The larger the diameter of the spinning, the darker red and the more impulsive the person. When the pendulum is spinning over the root chakra on the ethereal " double" image in clockwise circles, in a diameter of about a half of an inch, you are assessing the energy of a warm and generous person. When the root chakra needs healing and cleansing, a red colored pencil may be used to color this chakra and spirals to withdraw bad energy.

When your pendulum is spinning clockwise with a small diameter over the sacral chakra, it means that the drawn person has low energy, may feel tired, and needs an orange energy boost. When the sacral chakra needs healing and cleansing, coloring it with orange may be helpful. *Draw spirals from the sacral chakra withdrawing blocked or negative energy with an orange pencil as well.*

Perform assessment of all chakras using characteristics of colors and correct their work with needed colors.

Chapter Eight

Ether "Double" Image Crystal Healing

Healing Power of Crystals and Gemstones

Crystals and gemstones have been valued in many cultures for their healing and spiritual properties. Crystals and gemstones amaze with their orderliness and magnificence; they are the most systematic matter in the universe. Being physical matter, crystals and gemstones possess universal energy, which can bring harmony and healing to our bio-energetic systems. Crystals and gemstones have always been used to restore balance to the human bodies. According to ancient teachings of chakra healing with crystals, placing crystals over chakras bring healing and harmony to chakras. In today's stressful climate, we can especially benefit from a boost of this magic harmony to our chakra systems.

Putting the crystals into an unbalanced energetic system may bring coherence and vigor and overall orderliness restoring, balance. Crystals transferring their pure energy to already cleansed chakras achieve effective healing, whether it is a physical illness or an emotional or mental disturbance. The powerful energy of crystals helps our chakra systems to reinstate our own harmonious patterns of health.

Placing crystals over chakras will not only heal chakras, but maintain healthy subtle bodies as well. Placing crystals over chakras maintains a flow of energetic information and energy between subtle energetic bodies. Crystals' energy can help keep our bio-energy fields systematized, clarified, and luminously glowing.

Preference of Ether "Double" Image Crystal Healing

Many healers use crystals in chakra cleansing and balancing by placing them on the physical body. They feel that crystals alone are able to clarify chakras and help to release bad energy, restoring the whole subtle body system. However, crystals tend to accumulate bio-negative energy rather than release it. Their effectiveness can lessen, and they may bring feelings of heaviness or unpleasantness, or pass imbalances or energetic stagnation back into the system. In cases of placing the crystals over still-closed or blocked or dysfunctional chakras, crystals by themselves are in demand of constant and heavy cleansing with sea salt and charging with sunlight in order to be effective; the healing process may even require interruption to cleanse the crystals again. This procedure of healing and cleansing takes a long time and demands the presence of healee. Often we just do not have time to perform crystal healing on our physical bodies. Moreover, crystals need to be large in size in order to be effective on the physical body, and this is costly and uncomfortable.

Because of the reasons above, our method of the ether "double" image crystal healing seems to be the ultimate in usefulness. We use crystals on the ethereal "double" matrix, which does not require the direct participation of the healee. To greatly increase the effectiveness of crystals and gemstone, cleanse chakras (if needed) before placing crystals. In this way, whether once or rarely cleansed, crystals may bring balance and harmony for a long time.

For work with the ether "double" image drawing, we need surprisingly small crystals, which will work on the image as well as larger crystals do on the physical body. The course of healing may be prolonged as long as it is needed to heal any disturbed energetic condition.

Procedure of Ether "Double"
Crystal Healing

Draw your own or anyone's ether "double" image, and write the energetic identification on the top of the drawing. Assess the energetic state of all chakras with your pendulum. If all chakras are functioning normally, you may place crystals over the drawn chakras to achieve a desired energetic state or characteristics, which will be discussed later. If some chakras are closed or blocked, you need to draw spirals leading the blocking energy or negative information out of the chakras. As usual, end spirals with arrows inside the squares.

Be aware of the interrelation of chakras when conducting crystal healing. If you place a crystal on the root chakra, you should place it on the third eye chakra as well. The sacral chakra and the throat chakra are also interrelated, so crystals need to be placed on both of them as well. Finally, both the solar plexus and the heart chakra together need crystals for healing because of their interrelation. As you place a stone on the cleansed chakra on the energetic "double" image, the whole chakra's area will be influenced in a positive energetic way.

At the beginning of work with crystals, we advise putting crystals on all chakras for the best consequence of healing - seeking overall balance in chakras, the chakra's areas and the whole bio-energetic system. After balance in the chakra system is achieved, you may fix any imbalances in the physical body by placing a crystal over the drawn chakra, the place of pain or any temporary energetic disturbance. *Do not forget to throw away stagnant energy from a problem area before placing the crystal. Draw spirals from all chakras leading bio-negative energy away, and put stones on each chakra according to the color of the chakra and the color and desired characteristics of the stones.*

Whether your crystals are new or used, you need to cleanse them of any unwanted or harmful energy before use, restoring them to their original energetic state. For this purpose, *crystals may be buried in dry salt or sea salt for a while, then placed in direct sunlight.*

Or, you can quickly and effectively cleanse crystals with **"activated" energetic hands**. With activated bio-energy in your hands, you will be able to remove unwanted energy from white paper (for drawing the ether image) and from your crystals as well. To learn how to activate healing energy in your hands, open and develop pathways of bio-energy existing on the fingertips, and start feeling your own energy flow, you may perform the following exercises.

Activation of Healing Energy in Hands

1. *Spread your fingers apart, then bend them as if you are holding a ball. Start to "bounce" your palms until one thumb enters the space between the thumb and fingers of your other hand (like a horseshoe enters the space inside another horseshoe). Produce these movements to achieve a feeling of energy flow between your hands that feels like unseen woven energetic threads.*

2. *Concentrate your attention on the left hand, feel its warmth, weight, and sensation. Mentally move a visualized ball of concentrated energy from the left hand through the shoulders to the right hand transferring the energetic ball with your eyes, and then do this process backwards.*

3. *You may also "activate" the energy of your hands with static electricity. Still "holding a visualized ball" with one hand, spin it in a clockwise direction around the palm of the other motionless hand without touching each other.*

4. *Place your hands about six inches apart with palms facing each other. Start to "bounce" them, first bringing them close together and then far apart without touching. Keep moving them as if you would play catch. Feel your energy flow between the fingers of both hands.*

Perform the exercises as long as you need to feel the energy flow in your hands, which may be indicated by tingling, little shocks, warmth, coldness, or any other sensation showing the activating of the hands' energy.

Now you may remove negative energetic information from the crystals with your **"activated" hand**. *Make spiral movements in a clockwise direction with your "activated" hand starting over the crystal, leading negative energy out of the crystal and down. Repeat these spiral movements 5-10 times. At the end of your movements, shake the "activated" hand to throw away any negative energetic signals. Placing your hands over the crystals, move the hands up and down three times to remove any excess energy and to balance energy.* If you have kept your crystals in salt, you should throw away any left negative signal with spiral movements of your "activated" hand as well.

When you have prepared the ether "double" energetic image with drawn spirals and crystals, you may put crystals of appropriate colors and properties over chakras accordingly. Healed with its matching crystal, the chakra receives a boost of its own color vibration without altering its energy or the overall harmony of the whole system. To place crystals properly, we need some information on crystals and gemstones and their properties.

Properties of Crystals and Gemstones

The most important guideline in relating crystals to chakras is **color**, as well as **intuition** and **knowledge**. Here are some suggestions on selecting specific crystals.

Dark, Red, Black, and Smoky Stones (Root Chakra)

Red or dark stones promote centering and grounding effects, and earthiness. Red crystals play a regenerative and purifying role for flesh or tissue or blood. They help to calm fear and panic. Red crystals are good stimulators, activators, and energizers. They give an ability to use practical tools, help movement, activity, action, and physical survival, and protect physical existence.

Here are some crystals and gemstones to put on the root chakra.

Ruby, Corundum or **Carbunculus** is very bright in clear strong light. It brings vitality, energy, life force, and optimism. It shows strength of leadership and individuality. It is helpful in meditation.

Dark Tourmaline, Rubellite or **Schorl** brings pain relief and encourages new perspectives.

Red Garnet, Pyrope, Almandine, Hessonite or **Spessartite** brings focus and order and guides one to peace and clarity of mind. It is a good talisman.

Moss, red, black or dark smoky **Agate, Onyx, Jasper** or **Chalcedony** brings perseverance, encouraging, grounding, and energizing. It is a good talisman as well.

Black Opal is the most valuable specimen among silicon dioxides. It is helpful in bringing dynamics to the root chakra.

Smoky Quartz, Morion or dark **Rutilated Quartz** brings positive reassuring, security, and commitment to others. It eases depression and opens the mind to new possibilities.

Dark Bloodstone stimulates and connects to the earth.

Black or red **Obsidian, Haematite**, or **Pyrite** absorbs light and excess energy.

Orange and Light Brown
Stones (Sacral Chakra)

Orange or light brown stones bring an energy boost, courage, soothing, focusing, balancing, and healing on the physical and ether levels. Orange stones have qualities of mixed red and yellow, so their energizing effect is gentler and more appropriate than that of red stones. They help lift depression, heighten emotional maturity, bring healing to the organs of the lower abdomen, and heal wounded emotions and sexual problems. They will restore natural vitality and promote an energy increase.

Carnelian is the most powerful healer of the ether body. It brings positive motivation and eases stress and anxiety. Carnelian is a great talisman and aids in meditation.

Orange **Amber** helps relieve fatigue, helps one cope with daily struggles, and strengthens the spirit. It is a healthy energizer.

Dark **Citrine** or **Topaz** promotes tolerance and peace and increases energy.

Fire **Opal** has been highly prized since antiquity. It invigorates the decision-making process and encourages creativity and new ways.

Other important orange stones are **Calcite**, **Copper**, **Coral**, orange **Onyx**, light brown **Tourmaline**, **Rutilated Quartz**, and orange **Garnet**.

Yellow Stones (Solar Plexus Chakra)

Yellow stones are very good stimulants and regulators of the digestive, nervous, and immune systems. They are healers of emotions and psychic developers. Warmly colored, they promote and increase energy. As actual sunlight, yellow stones help heal the solar plexus and metabolism. They help the astral body to be healthy and powerful. Yellow stones also help in the development of personal identification.

Yellow **Topaz** or **Citrine** (fire in Sanskrit) is a precious gemstone, bringing personal wisdom and psychic-intuition. It helps in memorization and is a good sleep aid.

Yellow **Amber** boosts energy and memory. It has been highly valued since ancient times.

Yellow **Tourmaline** balances energy and helps relieve insomnia.

Tiger's Eye brings a harmonizing effect. It helps to unite will and desire and enhances self-confidence. It helps dreams to become reality, and is a good talisman and meditation helper.

Yellow **Rutilated Quartz** aids in the development of personal potential.

Yellow **Onyx** causes a stabilizing, healing and balancing effect.

Yellow **Jadeite** brings soothing and tranquil qualities. It promotes good judgement, emotional understanding and wisdom.

Golden Pyrite works as a yellow stone. It is a grounding force for commitment and energy. It is also a good regulator of digestive problems.

Green Stones (Heart Chakra)

Green stones have always been considered as the most magical and mystical gems. Green (a blend of yellow and blue) stones balance emotions and relationships, and give mental clarity. Green stones stimulate and harmonize the entire energy system. Green stones regulate communication between head, heart, and mental body, and heal allergies and asthma. Green gems revitalize all energies and increase vitality and longevity. They resonate serenity, wisdom, harmony, and peace with others.

Emerald is a precious gemstone. It maintains balance, self-esteem, and enhances memory. It brings a soothing and encouraging effect, inspiration, and spiritual growth.

Peridot, **Olivine** or **Chrysolite** brings a revitalizing and purifying effect for the mental body. It acts as a tonic to perplexed emotions, eases stress and anxiety, keeps in touch with the inner-self, and motivates personal growth and change.

Green **Bloodstone**, **Chalcedony** or **Heliotrope** helps to question the inner-self.

Chrysoprase or green **Chalcedony** balances and soothes energies. It eases stress and anxiety, and promotes creativity and intuition. It helps one to focus on the future without fear.

Malachite promotes understanding. It provides insight into the nature of fear, anxieties and guilt. It gives courage, strength, patience, and endurance. Malachite as a copper relieves pain. It is also a good absorber of bio-negative energy.

Alexandrite or **Chryoberyl** is a rare gemstone. It changes color from light green to rose under bright light right before your eyes. It promotes confidence, insight, refreshes body and spirit, and encourages positive thinking.

Green **Aventurine** regenerates energies. It strengthens will, brings sense of purpose, and encourages creativity and intuition.

Nephrite or **Jade** brings tranquility, soothing, understanding, and wisdom.

Green **Jasper** balances and heal energies.

Green **Tourmaline** or **Verdelite** boosts confidence in self-expression.

Green **Beryl** or **Aquamarine** balances and improves self-image, inner quiet, and tranquility.

Moonstone invites logic and intuition. It is a feminine stone. It balances emotion, desire, or oversensitivity.

Green **Rhodochrosite** inspires compassion and enhances friendship.

Pink Stones (Root or Heart Chakra)

Pink stones (a blend of red and white) are related to the root chakra and the heart chakra. They bring a calming and reassuring effect.

Rose **Quartz** brings a soothing effect. It promotes compassion, love, and a sense of relaxation. It is a gentle, nurturing, and feminine stone. It encourages imagination, reduces fear, and relaxes and calms the body.

Rhodochrosite (its name comes from Greek "rodon," meaning rose) brings a reconnecting effect and hope. It inspires forgiveness, compassion, and friendship.

Rhodonite helps to remove past feelings, bringing one into the present. It is a grounding force for commitment.

Pink **Topaz** brings inspiration. It promotes peace and endurance.

Blue Stones (Throat Chakra)

Blue stones strengthen the throat chakra in transpersonal expression and in connections to the higher-self, spirit and soul. They emphasize responsibility, self-expression, and great communication with others. They help connect intellect and abstract thought, in the impressing of ideas and expressing ideologies. They ease fears and phobias.

Blue **Aquamarine** or **Beryl** brings a purifying effect and strengthens perception, awareness, and courage.

Blue **Sapphire** brings healing, peace, and sureness, and strengthens the throat chakra.

Turquoise or **Callais** brings a connection to the higher-self. It is a favorite stone of American Indians. It is used to calm healing energy, is good for immune system, and enhances communication and loyalty.

Lazurite helps in the search for truth. It enables clearer communication skills and better focusing and understanding of ideas.

Blue Lace Agate brings healing and calming.

Blue **Sodalite** aids friendship, tolerance, and expression.

Blue **Opal** is a stone of truth and justice.

Blue **Tourmaline** or **Indicolite** boosts confidence in communication.

Indigo or Dark Blue Stones
(Third Eye Chakra)

Indigo or dark blue stones help perception, intuition, and understanding. They encourage spirit, completeness, awareness, inspiration, and insight. They help the hormonal balance. Indigo stones promote altered states of consciousness, provide protection from negative thinking, and bring harmony and peace to the mind. They decrease the bridge between personality and spirit, and help to emphasize a mental command.

Lapis Lazuli brings intellectual clarity, observance, and creativity.

Azurite brings clarifying and revealing effects. It aids in communication and promotes kindness.

Sodalite brings connecting and easing factors. It promotes understanding and clarity. It eases fear of the future and deepens thoughts.

Dark blue **Sapphire** brings good fortune, peace of mind, spiritual faith, and longevity. It has mystical properties.

Dark blue **Opal** encourages creativity and a desire to try new ways.

Selenite or **Gypsum** has meditative properties. It is often used in spiritual rituals as a spiritual guide and receptor. It promotes mental energy flow and awareness.

Clear or White Stones
(Crown Chakra)

Clear or white stones are understood as balanced and perfected in wisdom. They bring inspiration, imagination, oneness, knowing, and empathy. White stones reflect the qualities of universality, purity, and clarity.

Diamond is the most valuable stone. It manifests universal truth. It is a great talisman and meditation help. It brings spiritual awareness, willpower, and courage.

Clear **Amethyst** or **Quartz** calms the mind, dissolves anxiety, brings clarity, wisdom, and higher potential. It is one of the most versatile healing stones. It is used for headaches, insomnia relief, and eases depression.

Clear **Alexandrite** refreshes the spirit, and brings spiritual insight.

Anchorite or colorless **Tourmaline** encourages new perspectives.

Selenite promotes awareness. It is a good meditation aid as well.

White precious **Opal** encourages new ways and brings universal truth.

Multicolored Stones

If you have a multicolored stone, observe the whole tone and consider it as the stone's color. **Opal**, **Azyrite**, **Malachite**, and **Labradorite** are seen as multicolored stones.

Epilogue

Effects of Practicing Ether "Double" Image Chakra Healing

If you have chosen to practice Ether "Double" Image healing, you will explore a one-of-a-kind healing practice that breathes fresh air into ancient chakra teachings. Through lots of work and fun, you will be rewarded with energy, health and longevity.

As you progress in this work, you will find yourself changing in many positive ways. You will discover a new understanding of the outer world and your inner-self, and the ability to control it consciously and "energetically." You will develop powerful inner strength and high self-esteem, empathy for others, and extraordinary perception and intuition. You may feel as if you are a newly born person with sixth sense - the bio-energy ability. You will be able to perceive the energy fields of all living things and assess the energetic health information of anyone.

You may relieve any personal distress easily on an everyday basis, and negative moods like depression will become a thing of the past due to your new, positive outlook and ability to control your thoughts. Your mind will be clear and alert. Your thoughts are healing, and your powerful healing energy will follow your thoughts. Your visualized images will be alive in their energy. Your mind will easily go into a meditative state for creativity and self-healing.

Once you have begun energetic work, your goal is to continue your energetic work and healer's development, always exploring and strengthening your abilities. May you open your own door to the Future of Medicine.

Bibliography

Bassano, Mary. *Healing with Music and Color.* York Beach, ME: Samuel Weiser, Inc., 1992.

Capra, Fritjof. *The Tao of Physics.* Boston: Shambhala Publications, Inc., 1991.

Dale, Cyndi. *New Chakras Healing.* St. Paul, MN: Llewellyn Publications, 1996.

Epstein, Gerald. *Healing Visualizations. Creating Health Through Imagery.* New York, NY: Bantam Books, 1989.

Gardner Cordon, Joy. *Color and Crystals. A Journey Trough the Chakras.* Freedom, CA: The Crossing Press, 1998.

Johari, Harish. *Chakras. Energy Centers of Transformation.* Rochester,Vermont: Destiny Books, 1987.

Judith, Anodea. *Wheels of Life. A User's Guide to the Chakra System.* St. Paul, MN: Llewellyn Worldwide, 1998.

Klotsche, Charles. *Color Medicine*. Sedona, AZ: Light Technology Publishing, 1997.

Leadbeater, C. W. *Le Plan Astral*. S. Petersburg, Russia: Bogushevsky Publishing, 1908.

Leadbeater, C. W. *Mental Plan*. S. Petersburg, Russia: Publishing Labor, 1912.

Liberman, Jacob. *Light Medicine of the Future*. Santa Fe, NM: Bear & Company, Inc., 1991.

Lilly, Simon. *Crystals and Crystal Healing*. New York, NY: Lorenz Books, 1998.

Nudel, Michael and Nudel, Eva. *Health by Bio-Energy and Mind*. Los Angeles, CA: Bio-Energy System Services, 2000.

Ozaniec, Naomi. *The Elements of Chakras*. Rockport, MA: Element Books Limited, 1990.

Paulson, Genevieve Lewis. *Kundalini and the Chakras. A Practical Manual*. St. Paul, MN: Llewellyn Worldwide, 1997.

Ritberger, Carol. *Your Personality, Your Health*. Carlsbad, CA: Hay House, Inc., 1998.

Sharamon, Shalila and Baginski, Bodo J. *The Chakra Handbook*. Wilmot, WI: Lotus Light Publications, 1997.

Sherwood, Keith. *Chakra Therapy for Personal Growth and Healing*. St. Paul, MN: Llewellyn Worldwide, 1998.

Wauters, Ambika. *Chakras and Their Archetypes. Uniting Energy Awareness and Spiritual Growth.* Freedom, CA: The Crossing Press, 1997.

Wauters, Ambika. *Healing with the Energy of the Chakras.* Freedom, CA: The Crossing Press, 1998.

White, Ruth. *Working with Your Chakras.* York Beach, ME: Samuel Weiser, Inc., 1993.